OF

DISCARD

The Waco Standoff

Nick Treanor, *Book Editor*

Daniel Leone, *President*
Bonnie Szumski, *Publisher*
Scott Barbour, *Managing Editor*

OPPOSING VIEWPOINTS® SERIES **AT ISSUE IN HISTORY**

GREENHAVEN
PRESS®

THOMSON
GALE

San Diego • Detroit • New York • San Francisco • Cleveland
New Haven, Conn. • Waterville, Maine • London • Munich

LIBRARY OF CONGRESS CATALOGING-IN-PUBLICATION DATA
The Waco standoff / Nick Treanor, book editor.
p. cm. — (At issue in history)
Includes bibliographical references and index.
ISBN 0-7377-1727-0 (lib. bdg. : alk. paper) —
ISBN 0-7377-1728-9 (pbk. : alk. paper)
1. Waco Branch Davidian Disaster, Tex., 1993. 2. Koresh, David, 1959–1993.
3. Branch Davidians. I. Treanor, Nick. II. Series.
BP605.B72W33 2003
976.4'284063—dc21   2002192864

Contents

Foreword

Historian Robert Weiss defines history simply as "a record and interpretation of past events." Both elements—record and interpretation—are necessary, Weiss argues.

> Names, dates, places, and events are the essence of history. But historical writing is not a compendium of facts. It consists of facts placed in a sequence to tell a connected story. A work of history is not merely a story, however. It also must analyze what happened and *why*—that is, it must interpret the past for the reader.

For example, the events of December 7, 1941, that led President Franklin D. Roosevelt to call it "a date which will live in infamy" are fairly well known and straightforward. A force of Japanese planes and submarines launched a torpedo and bombing attack on American military targets in Pearl Harbor, Hawaii. The surprise assault sank five battleships, disabled or sank fourteen additional ships, and left almost twenty-four hundred American soldiers and sailors dead. On the following day, the United States formally entered World War II when Congress declared war on Japan.

These facts and consequences were almost immediately communicated to the American people who heard reports about Pearl Harbor and President Roosevelt's response on the radio. All realized that this was an important and pivotal event in American and world history. Yet the news from Pearl Harbor raised many unanswered questions. Why did Japan decide to launch such an offensive? Why were the attackers so successful in catching America by surprise? What did the attack reveal about the two nations, their people, and their leadership? What were its causes, and what were its effects? Political leaders, academic historians, and students look to learn the basic facts of historical events and to read the intepretations of these events by many different sources, both primary and secondary, in order to develop a more complete picture of the event in a historical context.

In the case of Pearl Harbor, several important questions surrounding the event remain in dispute, most notably the role of President Roosevelt. Some historians have blamed his policies for deliberately provoking Japan to attack in order to propel America into World War II; a few have gone so far as to accuse him of knowing of the impending attack but not informing others. Other historians, examining the same event, have exonerated the president of such charges, arguing that the historical evidence does not support such a theory.

The Greenhaven At Issue in History series recognizes that many important historical events have been interpreted differently and in some cases remain shrouded in controversy. Each volume features a collection of articles that focus on a topic that has sparked controversy among eyewitnesses, contemporary observers, and historians. An introductory essay sets the stage for each topic by presenting background and context. Several chapters then examine different facets of the subject at hand with readings chosen for their diversity of opinion. Each selection is preceded by a summary of the author's main points and conclusions. A bibliography is included for those students interested in pursuing further research. An annotated table of contents and thorough index help readers to quickly locate material of interest. Taken together, the contents of each of the volumes in the Greenhaven At Issue in History series will help students become more discriminating and thoughtful readers of history.

Introduction

In the United States, most law enforcement happens at state and local levels. Most criminal laws, for instance, are enacted by state legislatures and enforced by state troopers, sheriffs and their deputies, and city police. There are, however, numerous federal agencies that have a role in law enforcement, including the Federal Bureau of Investigation (FBI) and the Bureau of Alcohol, Tobacco, and Firearms (BATF), both of which were involved in the Waco standoff in the spring of 1993. Unlike city and state police officers, who work closely with the general public, the federal agents who work for these bureaus have little contact with ordinary citizens. Consequently, the purpose of these agencies and the work they do is not always clear to the average American. Yet these two agencies have been at the center of criticisms levied against them, and controversies over what happened at Waco fit into a pattern of criticism that emerged during the 1990s.

The Bureau of Alcohol, Tobacco, and Firearms

This bureau is a relatively young one, having been created in 1972. As an agency of the Treasury Department, the BATF is principally responsible for enforcing federal laws and regulations related to alcohol, tobacco, firearms, explosives, and arson and for collecting related taxes and fees. Although it was officially created only recently, it traces its roots back to 1789, when the first Congress under the new Constitution voted to impose a tax on imported spirits to offset its portion of the Revolutionary War debt. Impressed with the results, lawmakers included domestic spirits two years later, and in 1794 grumbling over the new taxes led to the short-lived Whiskey Rebellion. Taxes on alcohol and tobacco came and went as needed until 1862, when Congress created the Office of Internal Revenue within the Treasury Department and charged it with responsibility for collecting taxes on distilled spirits and tobacco. The following year Congress authorized the hiring of three detectives to prevent, detect, and punish tax evaders, thus bringing tax collecting and enforcement under one roof. The BATF, which is responsible for this collecting and enforcement, separated from the Office of Internal Revenue in 1972 and became an agency in its own right.

Today the agents, inspectors, and support staff of the BATF are "involved in investigating some of the most violent crimes in society, in regulating some of the most important and sensitive industries in America, and in collecting over $13 billion in annual revenue."[1] The bureau became involved at Waco after the local police contacted it, claiming that the Mount Carmel center was receiving regular shipments of gun parts and other materials that could be used in the production of machine guns and explosive grenades. The goal of the initial raid on February 28, 1993, was to search the Davidian property for evidence of illegal activity and to arrest David Koresh, who was known to be the leader of the organization.

The Federal Bureau of Investigation

The FBI is better known to most Americans than the BATF, mostly because it is regularly featured on television shows and in Hollywood movies, although the portrayal is not always accurate. The FBI is the main investigative arm of the Department of Justice and is authorized to investigate all federal criminal violations that have not been specifically assigned by Congress to another agency (and thus it is the broadest of all federal investigative agencies). In addition to investigating violations of federal criminal law, the FBI investigates terrorism and foreign intelligence activity within the United States and assists other federal, state, and local law enforcement agencies. Founded in 1908, the bureau has its headquarters in Washington and has fifty-six field offices, eleven thousand special agents, and sixteen thousand professional support personnel.

The FBI became involved at Waco shortly after the failed initial raid, which resulted in the deaths of six Branch Davidians and four BATF agents. FBI presence included both a tactical team, consisting of a heavily armed sniper and assault force, and negotiators, who were involved in hundreds of hours of telephone conversation with David Koresh and others inside Mount Carmel.

Although numerous controversies have arisen in regard

to the fifty-one-day standoff, most of the complaints boil down to two issues that concern whether the federal agencies involved abused their discretionary power: Did the BATF and FBI overreact to the situation with a gung ho, military-style approach? And were the Davidians treated unfairly because of their unusual religious beliefs?

An Overreaction?

Although some dispute that the BATF had legitimate reason to take a closer look at the activities of the Branch Davidians, it was certainly within the bureau's responsibilities to do so. The Davidians were receiving regular, large shipments of gun parts and other items that could be used to manufacture illegal weapons, and some activities at Mount Carmel, such as the posting of armed guards, could reasonably be thought to resemble the kinds of activities most often associated with criminal organizations. A more plausible criticism is that the bureau mismanaged its investigation and seriously overreacted when it sent nearly one hundred heavily armed agents to storm the Davidian center, a building containing men, women, and children of all ages. As Stuart A. Wright, a professor of sociology at Lamar University in Texas, points out in his book *Armageddon at Waco*, "It appears that no attempts were made by the federal agents to secure less violent or more peaceable means of enforcing the law. The deployment of excessive force appears to be the only option ever considered by BATF."[2]

The accusation that federal authorities overreacted and used excessive force continued after the initial raid, when the FBI took control of the scene and deployed its tactical team and its negotiators. While the negotiators talked with Koresh and other Davidians by telephone, the huge tactical team surrounded the building with heavily armed agents and military-grade tactical equipment. Ultimately, after tiring of negotiating and finding little success with pressure techniques, which included cutting off electricity to the center and blasting it with amplified noise throughout the night, the FBI pumped large amounts of a potent tear gas into the building in an apparent effort to drive out the Davidians. This last technique precipitated the tragic fire that killed seventy-six Branch Davidians, including twenty-one children. Even the earlier techniques were criticized as counterproductive by the FBI negotiating team.

Unfair Treatment?

The second general theme that characterizes the specific criticisms raised about the federal handling of the incident at Waco concerns whether the Branch Davidians were treated unfairly because of their religious beliefs. The Davidian faith is based on traditional Christian teachings but adds new elements, the most important of which is that David Koresh is a prophet of God. (Some media mistakenly reported that Koresh thought he was Jesus Christ.) Whatever the exact details of their religious beliefs may have been, the Davidians showed little interest in converting others and preferred to keep to themselves, living in relative isolation.

Both the BATF and the FBI labeled the Davidians not as a *religious movement* but as a *cult*, a dismissive term that suggests the Davidians' beliefs were not to be taken seriously and that the Davidians themselves were irrational or deluded in holding them. This perspective may also have influenced the planning of the initial raid and the FBI negotiation strategy. The application for a search warrant, for instance, contains numerous references to the Davidians' religious beliefs and to other unusual beliefs or practices within the group, even though there was no connection between these beliefs and practices and the substantial allegations contained in the document. Similarly, throughout the negotiations the FBI consistently referred to Koresh's theological discussions as "Bible babble," even though respected religious scholars said his religious pronouncements constituted a coherent system and evinced considerable scholarship. Whereas some religious scholars thought Koresh could be reasoned with if one accepted his religious framework for the purposes of the discussion, the FBI dismissed him as probably insane.

A Pattern of Criticism

The controversy over the abuse of discretionary power at Waco is just part of the many criticisms that were leveled during the 1990s. The Waco standoff was seen not as an isolated incident in which federal agents lost their cool, but as part of a recurrent abuse of the public trust.

In the years preceding the Waco standoff, for instance, several high-profile cases showed that federal law enforcement cracked down with apparent ruthlessness on people with aberrant or unpopular views who were suspected, sometimes on flimsy evidence, of having committed crimes. One such case was that of Randy Weaver, a white separatist who lived in the backwoods of Idaho with his wife and son. Along with being racist, Weaver adhered to his own religious views, which emphasized a literal interpretation of the Bible, and he believed the government intruded far too much into people's lives. The Weaver family lived "off the grid," in a rustic cabin cobbled together out of plywood and spare pieces of lumber, and supported itself by growing its own vegetables and hunting game. Although there is no evidence he was ever involved in ongoing criminal activity, Randy Weaver had on one occasion agreed to illegally shorten a shotgun at the request of an undercover agent and was put under intense surveillance after he failed to appear at the scheduled trial date. By late in the summer of 1992, U.S. marshals planning his arrest had conducted over twenty surveillance missions and had compiled hundreds of hours of clandestine videos of Weaver and his family.

A final surveillance mission on August 21, conducted by three U.S. marshals dressed in camouflage and armed with a shotgun, a .223 caliber M-16, and a 9mm submachine gun equipped with a silencer, led to tragedy. Although the three marshals had been ordered to proceed "under cover of darkness"[3] and to avoid provoking a confrontation, shortly after 10 A.M., as they approached the Weaver home, one of them tossed rocks toward the family's dogs to see how they would respond. The dogs began barking and one, which was unchained, gave chase. Randy Weaver, along with his son, Sammy, a slight fourteen-year-old who weighed less than eighty pounds, and Kevin Harris, a family friend, ran out of the house with their guns to investigate. The three followed the dog into the woods, apparently in the hope that it was after a deer. When Weaver, who had taken a different trail than the other two, saw the marshals, he turned around and hurried back to the house.

Although there is no agreement on the exact sequence of events, within a few minutes the marshals had killed both the dog and Weaver's son, who was shot in the back as he ran toward the house; Harris had shot and killed one of the marshals. Soon thereafter, with Harris and the Weaver family grieving in the cabin and the two marshals huddled around their colleague's body a half mile away, word reached Washington that a federal marshal had been murdered and two others were pinned down by hostile fire from armed fanatics. Just as it would at Waco a half year later, the FBI mobilized its crack Hostage Rescue Team and rushed to the scene.

Before long, the ramshackle Weaver cabin—now dubbed a mountain stronghold by the government—was surrounded by hundreds of FBI agents and other law enforcement officers, including fifty-one antiterrorist snipers and assault commandos. The rules of engagement for the standoff gave the snipers the authority to kill, without warning, any armed adult they saw. By the end of the following day, both Weaver and Harris had been shot and wounded, and Weaver's wife, Vicki, was shot in the head and killed as she stood in the doorway holding the couple's baby. Throughout the siege, Weaver had not fired a single shot at anyone.

A Bloody Symbol

Like the Waco standoff, in the eyes of many the siege at Ruby Ridge and its tragic ending pointed to serious problems in American law enforcement. As the *New York Times* noted in 1995, "The incident has become a deep embarrassment for the F.B.I. and a bloody symbol of excessive law enforcement. . . . It has been seen as a case in which the authorities used military-style tactics to terrorize a rural malcontent initially accused of a relatively minor crime."[4] Although Weaver held views most people considered warped, it was unclear why the government had devoted such enormous energy to investigating him and had provoked such a bloody confrontation. A high-ranking Justice Department official told the *Washington Post* in 1995, "Weaver wasn't bothering anyone. If the government hadn't messed with him, he'd still be up on that mountain, talking nonsense."[5]

The "dynamic entry" search and arrest warrant issued in Waco ultimately led to eighty-four deaths, including those of four federal agents and of numerous people inside the Davidian center who could not conceivably have been thought to have caused anyone harm. The enormously intricate plan to arrest Randy Weaver, who was suspected of nothing more than a minor offense and later acquitted of that charge, ultimately led to the death of a federal marshal and of Weaver's wife and fourteen-year-old son, neither of whom was even subject to investigation. Such incidents, and others like them, raise the question of whether they represent a serious abuse of discretionary power or merely bad luck on the part of federal law enforcement agencies. Whether government abuses its power is at the heart of the content in *At Issue in History: The Waco Standoff.* The authors of the following articles represent a variety of views on the topic.

Notes
1. Bureau of Alcohol, Tobacco, and Firearms website, www. atf.treas.gov.
2. Stuart A. Wright, ed., *Armageddon at Waco: Critical Perspectives on the Branch Davidian Conflict*. Chicago: University of Chicago Press, 1995, pp. 76–77.
3. George Lardner Jr. and Richard Leiby, "Standoff at Ruby Ridge: Botched 'Anti-Terrorist' Operation Began with Series of Overreactions," *Washington Post*, September 3, 1995, pp. 1–3.
4. David Johnson, "Teary-Eyed White Separatist Recalls FBI Slaying of Wife," *New York Times*, September 7, 1995, p. 14.
5. Lardner and Leiby, "Standoff at Ruby Ridge," p. 1.

Chapter 1

The Seven Week Standoff

1

The Davidian Home Raid Is Necessary

Davy Aguilera

The following piece is an excerpt from the affidavit sworn by
Davy Aguilera on February 25, 1993, in an application for a
warrant to search Mount Carmel, the Branch Davidian center
in Waco. Aguilera, a special agent for the Bureau of Alcohol,
Tobacco, and Firearms, describes his investigation of Koresh
and the other Branch Davidians and argues that there are
probable grounds to believe that they are unlawfully manufacturing and possessing machine guns and explosives. Aguilera
cites the large number of gun parts that had been delivered to
Mount Carmel, as well as reports of other activities he consid-
ers suspicious.

I, Davy Aguilera, being duly sworn, depose and state that:
I am a Special Agent with the U.S. Treasury Department, Bureau of Alcohol, Tobacco and Firearms, Austin,
Texas, and I have been so employed for approximately 5
years. This affidavit is based on my own investigation as well
as information furnished to me by other law enforcement
officers and concerned citizens. . . .

On June 4, 1992, I met with Lieutenant Gene Barber,
McLennan County Sheriff's Department, Waco, Texas,
who has received extensive training in explosives classification, identification and the rendering safe of explosive de-

Davy Aguilera, "Affidavit, February 25, 1993," *Activities of Federal Law Enforcement
Agencies Toward the Branch Davidians: Part I, Joint Hearings Before the Subcommittee on
Crime of the Committee of the Judiciary, House of Representatives, and the Subcommittee
on National Security, International Affairs, and Criminal Justice of the Committee on
Government Reform and Oversight, 104th Congress, First Session, July 19, 20, 21, and
24, 1995*. Washington, DC: U.S. Government Printing Office, 1996, pp. 996–1,010.

vices and has been recognized in Federal Court as an expert witness in this field. Lt. Barber stated that he had received information in May 1992, from an employee of United Parcel Service, Waco, Texas, that from April through June of 1992, several deliveries had been made to a place known as the "Mag-Bag", Route 7, Box 555-B, Waco, Texas, 76705, located on Farm Road number 2491, in the names of Mike Schroeder and David Koresh, which the UPS employee believed to be firearms components and explosives. Through my investigation, I know that the place known as the "Mag-Bag" is a small tract of land located at the above address which has two metal buildings located on it.

The name "Mag-Bag" comes from the shipping label which accompanied many items shipped to the above address. I and other agents have personally observed vehicles consistently over the past six months at the "Mag-Bag" location which are registered to Vernon Wayne Howell, aka: David Koresh. Lieutenant Barber further stated that the UPS employee, Larry Gilbreath, became suspicious and concerned about the deliveries, most of which were shipped Cash On Delivery, (C.O.D.) because of their frequency and because of the method used by the recipient to receive the shipments and to pay for them.

Suspicious Deliveries

Lieutenant Barber explained that David Koresh was an alias name used by Vernon Wayne Howell who operated a religious cult commune near Waco, Texas, at a place commonly known as the Mount Carmel Center, which is one of the premises to be searched and more specifically described above. I have learned from my investigation, particularly from my discussions with former cult members that Vernon Howell adopted the name David Koresh more than a year ago. The name "David Koresh" was chosen by Howell because Howell believed that the name helped designate him as the messiah or the anointed one of God. Lieutenant Barber further related that he was told by Gilbreath that he has been making deliveries to the "Mag-Bag" and the Mount Carmel Center on Double EE Ranch Road, Waco, Texas, for several years, but he had never been suspicious of any of the deliveries until 1992. Gilbreath became concerned because he made several C.O.D. deliveries addressed to the "Mag-Bag", but when he would stop at that location he was instructed to wait while a telephone call was made to the Mount Carmel Center by the person at the "Mag-Bag", usually Woodrow Kendrick or Mike Schroeder, notifying the person who answered the phone at the Mount Carmel Center that UPS was coming there with a C.O.D. delivery, after which Gilbreath would be instructed to drive to the Mount Carmel Center to deliver the package and collect for it. That on those occasions when he was at the Mount Carmel Center to deliver and collect for the C.O.D. packages. He saw several manned observation posts, and believed that the observers were armed. . . .

On July 21, 1992, I met with Robert L. Cervenka, Route 7, Box 103, Riesel, Texas. Mr. Cervenka farms the property surrounding the east side of the Mount Carmel property. Mr. Cervenka stated that he has farmed that area since 1948. From about January and February of 1992 he has heard machinegun fire on the Vernon Howell property during the night hours. He is familiar with and knows the sound of machinegun fire because he did a tour overseas with the U.S. Army. He believes that some of the gunfire he heard was being done with 50 caliber machineguns and possibly M-16 machineguns. . . .

The Mount Carmel Weapons Cache

As a result of my investigation of shipments to Howell/ Koresh and Mike Schroeder at the "Mag-Bag" Corporation, Waco, Texas, through the United Parcel Service, and the inspection of the firearms records of Henry McMahon, dba, Hewitt Hand Guns, Hewitt, Texas, I have learned that they acquired during 1992, the following firearms and related explosive paraphernalia:

> One hundred four (104), AR-15/M-16, upper receiver groups with barrels.
> Eight thousand, one hundred (8,100) rounds of 9mm and .223 caliber ammunition for AR-15/M-16.
> Twenty (20), one hundred round capacity drum magazines for AK-47 rifles.
> Two hundred sixty (260), M-16/AR-15, magazines.
> Thirty (30) M-14, magazines.
> Two (2) M-16 EZ kits.
> Two (2) M-16 Car Kits.
> One M-76 grenade launcher.

Two hundred (200) M-31, practice rifle grenades.
Four (4) M-16 parts set Kits "A".
Two (2) flare launchers.
Two cases, (approximately 50) inert practice hand
  grenades.
40–50 pounds of black gun powder.
Thirty (30) pounds of Potassium Nitrate.
Five (5) pounds of Magnesium metal powder.
One pound of Igniter cord. (A class C explosive)
Ninety-one (91) AR/15 lower receiver units.
Twenty-six (26) various calibers and brands of hand
  guns and long guns.
90 pounds of aluminum metal powder.
30–40 cardboard tubes.

The amount of expenditures for the above listed firearm paraphernalia, excluding the (91) AR-15 lower receiver units and the (26) complete firearms, was in excess of $44,300.

From my investigation, I have learned that a number of shipments to the "Mag-Bag" have been from vendors with questionable trade practices. One is presently under investigation by the Bureau of Alcohol, Tobacco and Firearms, for violations of the National Firearms Act, which prohibits unlawful possession of machineguns, silencers, destructive devices, and machinegun conversion kits. . . .

Alleged Sexual Abuse

On December 7, 1992, I spoke with Special Agent Carlos Torres, Bureau of Alcohol, Tobacco and Firearms, Houston, Texas, who had been assisting me in a portion of this investigation. He related to me the results of his interview on December 4, 1992, with Joyce Sparks, Texas Department of Human Services, Waco, Texas. Special Agent Torres told me that Ms. Sparks received a complaint from outside the State of Texas, that David Koresh was operating a commune type compound, and that he was sexually abusing young girls. Ms. Sparks stated that on February 27, 1992, she along with two other employees of the Texas Department of Human Services and two McLennan County Sheriff's Deputies responded to the complaint. They went to the Mount Carmel Center compound located east of Waco in McLennan County. When they arrived at the compound, they were met by a lady who identified herself as Rachel Koresh, the wife of David Koresh.

Mrs. Koresh was reluctant to talk with Ms. Sparks because David Koresh was not there. She had strict orders from him not to talk with anyone unless he was present. Ms. Sparks finally was able to convince Mrs. Koresh to allow her to talk with some of the children who were present. She talked to a young boy about 7 or 8 years old. The child said that he could not wait to grow up and be a man. When Ms. Sparks asked him why he was in such a hurry to grow up, he replied that when he grew up he would get a "long gun" just like all the other men there. When Ms. Sparks pursued the subject, the boy told her that all the adults had guns and that they were always practicing with them. . . .

Training for Violence

On December 11, 1992, I interviewed Robyn Bunds in LaVerne, California. Robyn Bunds is a former member and resident of Vernon Howell's commune in Waco, Texas. She told me that in 1988, at the age of 19, she gave birth to a son that was fathered by Vernon Howell. Her departure from the commune in 1990 was a result of Howell becoming progressively more violent and abusive.

While she was there, she and the other residents were subjected to watching extremely violent movies of the Vietnam war which Howell would refer to as training films. Howell forced members to stand guard of the commune 24 hours a day with loaded weapons. Howell always was in possession of firearms and kept one under his bed while sleeping. Robyn stated that her present residence in California belonged to her parents. For a period of several years Howell had exclusive control of the residence and used it for other members of his cult when they were in California. It was later relinquished by Howell to Robyn's mother. In June 1992, while she was cleaning one of the bedrooms of the residence she found a plastic bag containing gun parts. She showed them to her brother, David Bunds, who has some knowledge of firearms. He told her that it was a machinegun conversion kit. She stored the gun parts in her garage because she felt certain that Howell would send some of his followers to pick them up. Subsequent to her discovery of the conversion kit, Paul Fatta, Jimmy Riddle, and Neal Vaega, all members of Howell's cult and residents of the commune in Waco, came from Waco, Texas, to California and picked up the conversion kit.

Another Former Member Speaks

On December 12, 1992, I interviewed Jeannine Bunds, the mother of Robyn and David Bunds. She told me that she was a former member of Howell's group in Waco, Texas, having left there in September 1991. She is a registered nurse and was working in that capacity at the Good Samaritan Hospital, Los Angeles, California. While at Howell's commune in Waco, she participated in live fire shooting exercises conducted by Howell. She saw several long guns there, some of which she described as AK-47 rifles. Mrs. Bunds described the weapon to me and was able identify an AK-47 from among a number of photographs of firearms shown to her by me. I believe that she is well able to identify an AK-47. In July of 1991, she saw Howell shooting a machinegun on the back portion of the commune property. She knew it was a machinegun because it functioned with a very rapid fire and would tear up the ground when Howell shot it. Mrs. Bunds also told me that Howell had fathered at least fifteen (15) children from various women and young girls at the compound. Some of the girls who had babies fathered by Howell were as young as 12 years old. She had personally delivered seven (7) of these children.

According to Ms. Bunds, Howell annuls all marriages of couples who join his cult. He then has exclusive sexual access to the women. He also, according to Mrs. Bunds, has regular sexual relations with young girls there. The girls' ages are from eleven (11) years old to adulthood.

On January 6, 1993, I interviewed Jeannine Bunds again in Los Angeles, California. I showed her several photographs of firearms and explosives devices. She identified an AR-15 rifle and a pineapple type hand grenade as being items which she had seen at the Mount Carmel Center while she was there. She stated that she saw several of the AR-15 rifles and at least one of the hand grenades. . . .

During this investigation I made inquiries of a number of law enforcement data bases for information about those commune residents who I have been able to identify. Through TECS I learned that some forty (40) foreign nationals from Jamaica, United Kingdom, Israel, Australia and New Zealand have entered the United States at various times in the past and have used the address of the Mount Carmel Center, Waco, Texas, as their point of contact while here. According to INS records most of these foreign nationals have overstayed their entry permits or visas and are therefore illegally in the United States. I know that it is a violation of Title 18, United States Code, Section 922 for an illegal alien to receive a firearm. . . .

Illegal Explosives

On January 6, 1993, I received the results of an examination conducted by Jerry A. Taylor, Explosives Enforcement Officer, Bureau of Alcohol, Tobacco and Firearms, Walnut Creek, California, in response to a request from me to render an opinion on device design, construction, functioning, effects, and classification of explosives materials which have been accumulated by Howell and his followers. Mr. Taylor has received extensive training in Explosives Classification, Identification and rendering safe of explosive devices and has been recognized on numerous occasions as an expert witness in Federal Court. Mr. Taylor stated that the chemicals Potassium Nitrate, Aluminum, and Magnesium, when mixed in the proper proportions, do constitute an explosive as defined by Federal law. He further stated that Igniter cord is an explosive. Also Mr. Taylor stated that the inert practice rifle grenades and hand grenades would, if modified as weapons with the parts available to Howell, become explosives devices as defined by Federal law. Finally he stated that black powder is routinely used as the main charge when manufacturing improvised explosive weapons such as grenades and pipe bombs. I know that Title 26, United States Code, Section 5845 makes it unlawful for a person to possess any combination of parts designed or intended for use in converting any device into a destructive device. The definition of "firearm" includes any combination of parts, either designed or intended for use in converting any device into a destructive device such as a grenade, and from which a destructive device may be readily assembled. See *United States v. Price*, 877 F.2d 334 (5th Cir. 1989). So long as an individual possesses all of the component parts that constitutes a destructive device even though it is not assembled, so long as it can be readily assembled. *United States v. Russell*, 468 F.Supp. 322 (D.C. Tex. 1979).

On January 8, 1993, I interviewed Marc Breault in Los Angeles, California. He is an American citizen who lives in Australia with his wife Elizabeth. He was once a member of the "Branch Davidian" in Waco, Texas. He lived at the

Mount Carmel Center from early 1988 until September 1989. While there he participated in physical training and firearm shooting exercises conducted by Howell. He stood guard armed with a loaded weapon. Guard duty was maintained twenty-four (24) hours a day seven (7) days a week. Those who stood guard duty were instructed by Howell to "shoot to kill" anyone who attempted to come through the entrance gate of the Mount Carmel property. On one occasion, Howell told him that he wanted to obtain and/or manufacture machineguns, grenades and explosive devices. . . .

A Disturbing Pattern

On January 12, 1993, I spoke with Special Agent Earl Dunagan, Bureau of Alcohol, Tobacco and Firearms, Austin, Texas, who is assisting me in this investigation. He related the results of his inquiry to the ATF Firearms Technology Branch, Washington, D.C., for an opinion concerning the firearms parts which have been accumulated by Howell and his group. Special Agent Dunagan stated that he had spoken with Curtis Bartlett, Firearms Enforcement Officer, Washington, D.C., and was told by Officer Bartlett that the firearms parts which Howell has received and the method by which he has received them, is consistent with activities in other ATF investigations in various parts of the United States, which have resulted in the discovery and seizure of machineguns. Mr. Bartlett stated that the firearms parts received by Howell could be used to assemble both semi-automatic firearms and machineguns. He has examined many firearms which had been assembled as machineguns which included these type parts.

Mr. Bartlett also told Special Agent Dunagan that one of the vendors of supplies to Howell has been the subject of several ATF investigations in the past. ATF executed a search warrant at this Company and had seized a number of illegal machineguns and silencers. . . .

During his time at the Mount Carmel Center Mr. Block was present several occasions when Howell would ask if anyone had any knowledge about making hand grenades or converting semi-automatic rifles to machineguns. At one point he also heard discussion about a shipment of inert hand grenades and Howell's intent to reactivate them. Mr. Block stated that he observed at the compound published magazines such as, the "Shotgun News" and other related clandestine magazines. He heard extensive talk of the existence of the "Anarchist Cook Book". . . .

An Agent Undercover

On February 22, 1993, ATF Special Agent Robert Rodriguez told me that on February 21, 1993, while acting in an undercover capacity, he was contacted by David Koresh and was invited to the Mount Carmel compound. Special Agent Rodriguez accepted the invitation and met with David Koresh inside the compound. Vernon Howell, also known as David Koresh played music on a guitar for 30 minutes and then began to read the Bible to Special Agent Rodriguez. During this session, Special Agent Rodriguez was asked numerous questions about his life. After answering all the questions Special Agent Rodriguez was asked to attend a two week Bible session with David Koresh. This was for Special Agent Rodriguez to learn the 7 Seals and become a member of the group. Special Agent Rodriguez was told that by becoming a member he (Rodriguez) was going to be watched and disliked. David Koresh stated that Special Agent Rodriguez would be disliked because the Government did not consider the group religious and that he (Koresh) did not pay taxes or local taxes because he felt he did not have to. David Koresh told Special Agent Rodriguez that he believed in the right to bear arms but that the U.S. Government was going to take away that right. David Koresh asked Special Agent Rodriguez if he knew that if he (Rodriguez) purchased a drop-in-Sear for an AR-15 rifle it would not be illegal, but if he (Rodriguez) had an AR-15 rifle with the Sear that it would be against the law. David Koresh stated that the Sear could be purchased legally. David Koresh stated that the Bible gave him the right to bear arms. David Koresh then advised Special Agent Rodriguez that he had something he wanted Special Agent Rodriguez to see. At that point he showed Special Agent Rodriguez a video tape on ATF which was made by the Gun Owners Association (G.O.A.). This film portrayed ATF as an agency who violated the rights of Gun Owners by threats and lies.

I believe that Vernon Howell, also known as David Koresh and/or his followers who reside at the compound known locally as the Mount Carmel Center are unlawfully manufacturing and possessing machineguns and explosive devices.

2

The Davidian Home Should Not Have Been Raided

David B. Kopel and Paul H. Blackman

In the following piece, reprinted from the *Hamline Journal of Public Law and Policy*, David B. Kopel and Paul H. Blackman argue that the initial raid on Mount Carmel, the Branch Davidian home, was based on a deeply flawed search and arrest warrant. According to Kopel and Blackman, the warrant application filed by the Bureau of Alcohol, Tobacco, and Firearms contains many serious legal and factual errors. As they see it, no credible evidence was cited that either Koresh or the Branch Davidians were doing anything illegal. Furthermore, they argue that the raid was planned as a publicity stunt by the bureau, which had hoped to bolster its image in the public eye in advance of a congressional budget hearing. Kopel is research director of the Independence Institute and Blackman is research coordinator for the National Rifle Association's Institute for Legislative Action. Together they are the authors of *No More Wacos: What's Wrong with Federal Law Enforcement and How to Fix It*, Prometheus Books, 1997.

In mid-November 1992, personnel from the *60 Minutes* television program began contacting BATF [Bureau of Alcohol, Tobacco and Firearms] officials regarding a story that *60 Minutes* was producing about sexual harassment within the BATF. At the same time, the BATF knew that a

David B. Kopel and Paul H. Blackman, "The Unwarranted Warrant: The Waco Search Warrant and the Decline of the Fourth Amendment," *Hamline Journal of Public Law and Policy*, vol. 18, Fall 1996. Copyright © 1996 by *Hamline Journal of Public Law and Policy*. Reproduced by permission.

new President was coming to power—a President [Bill Clinton] who had pledged to fight sexual harassment on every front, to "reinvent government," and to cut the federal budget deficit.

The BATF had already been on the defensive about discrimination. In 1990, black agents had filed suit in federal court claiming that the BATF racially discriminated in hiring, promotion and evaluation. A fresh round of discrimination complaints by black BATF agents came in October 1992, the month before *60 Minutes* began setting up interviews for the sex discrimination story. The *60 Minutes* report, which would air on January 10, 1993, put the BATF in a vulnerable position for the Congressional budget hearing that would take place in early March, given the new administration's concern with sexual and racial harassment, and with reorganizing the government. . . .

The BATF had investigated David Koresh in the summer of 1992. The BATF investigation began about a month after an Australian tabloid television program produced a story about Koresh. Having lain moribund since the summer, the BATF investigation perked up in mid-November. By early December, the BATF was planning the raid on a seventy-seven acre property outside Waco, the Mount Carmel Center, which the Branch Davidians called their communal home.

A Publicity Stunt

A BATF memo written two days before the February 28, 1993, raid explained "this operation will generate considerable media attention, both locally [Texas] and nationally." The BATF public relations director, Sharon Wheeler, called reporters to ask them for their weekend phone numbers. The reporters contend, and Wheeler denies, that she asked them if they would be interested in covering a weapons raid on a "cult." Wheeler, on the other hand, states that she merely told them, "We have something going down." After the raid, the BATF at first denied there had been any media contacts. Journalist Ronald Kessler reports that the BATF told eleven media outlets that the raid was coming. The Department of the Treasury has refused to release the pre-raid memos which deal with publicity, asserting that they are exempt from the Freedom of Information Act.

In any case, the BATF's public relations officer was stationed in Waco on the day of the raid ready to issue a press release announcing the raid's success. A much-publicized raid, resulting in the seizure of hundreds of guns and dozens of "cultists" might reasonably be expected to improve the fortunes of BATF Director, Stephen Higgins, who was scheduled to testify before the U.S. Senate Appropriations Subcommittee on Treasury, Postal Service, and General Government on March 10, 1993. Investigative reporter Carol Vinzant wrote:

> In the jargon of at least one ATF office, the Waco raid was what is known as a ZBO ("Zee Big One"), a press-drawing stunt that when shown to Congress at budget time justifies more funding. One of the largest deployments in bureau history, the attack on the Branch Davidians compound was, in the eyes of some of the agents, the ultimate ZBO.

60 Minutes rebroadcast the BATF segment a few months later. Host Mike Wallace opined that almost all the agents he talked to said that they believe the initial attack on that cult in Waco was a publicity stunt—the main goal of which was to improve ATF's tarnished image. The code-word for the beginning of the BATF raid was "showtime."

The Initial Investigation

In June of 1992, an investigation began of possible violations of federal firearms laws by David Koresh and a few of his close associates. The justification for the initial investigation was that a United Parcel Service (UPS) driver reported to the McLennan County (Waco) Sheriff's Office several deliveries of firearms components and explosives which the driver considered suspicious.

The driver found it suspicious that some attempted deliveries to a place known as the Mag Bag, a garage rented by the Davidians near Waco, resulted in the driver being instructed to deliver the packages to Koresh's residence at the Mount Carmel Center. According to the UPS driver, his suspicions were heightened when boxes broke open by accident, and he could tell their contents were inert hand grenade hulls and a quantity of blackpowder. The Waco Sheriff's Office was informed of the "suspicious" deliveries, and the sheriff's office in turn notified the BATF.

Koresh had a number of raising funds schemes for the

Branch Davidians: mounting inert grenade hulls as plaques and selling them at gun shows was one of their biggest money-makers. Custom-sewn magazine vests in tall and big sizes, under the "David Koresh Brand" label, were another speciality. Koresh also used gun shows as a way to make a profit on selling surplus meals-ready-to-eat (MREs). In addition, the Davidians assembled gun parts into complete guns, which they sold to the public through a licensed dealer. The Davidians also bought many semi-automatic rifles as an investment, assuming that an anti-gun President would act in such a way as to increase their value dramatically; just as President George [Herbert Walker] Bush's ban on the import of such rifles had increased their value in 1989. On the day of the BATF attack, many of the Davidian guns were on display miles away at a gun show.

[60 Minutes] *host Mike Wallace opined that almost all the agents he talked to said that they believe the initial attack on that cult in Waco was a publicity stunt.*

While most guns owned by the Davidians were for investment purposes, the Davidians did own guns for protection. Koresh was concerned about a possible attack from George Roden, the former Branch Davidian leader, with whom Koresh and his followers had a shoot-out in 1987. Roden, who escaped from an institution for the criminally insane and was later recaptured, had reportedly threatened, "I'm not going to come back with BB guns." They also feared attacks from other persons who regularly sent hate mail to Koresh.

Ownership of machine guns in the United States is legal, but the owner must pay a federal tax and file a registration form with the Bureau of Alcohol, Tobacco and Firearms. The BATF's legal reason for the Branch Davidian investigation was to see if the Davidians were manufacturing machine guns illegally. If, on the other hand, Koresh had simply bought machine guns that were made before 1986, rather than allegedly manufacturing them, and if Koresh had paid the proper tax of $200 per gun and filed the appropriate paperwork, he would have been in full compliance with the law. In other words, the legal cause for the BATF investigation was not machine guns per se, but ownership or manufacturing of machine guns without registration and taxation. The seventy-six person BATF Mount Carmel raid was, ultimately, a tax collection case. . . .

Inaccurate Records

As part of the Branch Davidian investigation, the BATF checked its records to determine whether "Vernon Howell" (which was the birth name of the Branch Davidian prophet, who had been using the name "David Koresh" for the past several years) or Paul Fatta (who ran the Branch Davidian table at gun shows) had federal machine gun licenses. The BATF also checked its records to determine whether Vernon Howell, David Koresh, David Jones (one of Koresh's in-laws), or Paul Fatta were federally-licensed firearms dealers. The records said they were not.

On the other hand, the BATF knew that its records of registered machine gun owners were grossly incomplete. When a person is charged with possessing an unregistered machine gun, federal prosecutors call as a witness a BATF employee who testifies that the National Firearms Registration and Transfer Record (NFR&TR) database was checked, and the defendant was not listed as a registered machine gun owner. The federal database of machine gun owners, the NFR&TR, is maintained by the BATF. In October 1995, on a BATF agent training videotape, Thomas Busey, who was then head of the National Firearms Act Branch at the BATF, in charge of the machine gun records, made a startling admission. Busey explained, "when we testify in court, we testify that the database is one hundred percent accurate. That's what we testify to, and we will always testify to that. As you probably well know, that may not be one hundred percent true." He elaborated: "when I first came in a year ago, our error rate was between forty-nine and fifty percent, so you can imagine what the accuracy of the NFRTR could be, if your error rate's forty-nine to fifty percent. The error rate is now down below eight percent. . . ."

In other words, for many years BATF employees have testified many times per year in NFA prosecutions that the NFR&TR database is one hundred percent accurate. That testimony has been consistently false. . . .

Disrespect of the Constitution

The BATF investigation of Koresh quickly led to Henry McMahon, doing business as Hewitt Handguns, Koresh's favorite gun dealer. The lead BATF agent on the Koresh case, Davy Aguilera, listed in his affidavit for the search and arrest warrants all of the relatively recent purchases by Koresh, including flare launchers, over one hundred rifles, an M-76 grenade launcher, various kits, cardboard tubes, blackpowder, and practice grenades. All of those items may be lawfully owned without the government's permission. Accordingly, the purchases, while listed in the affidavit, did not in themselves establish probable cause that Koresh or his followers had violated or were planning to violate any federal law.

The BATF warrant application insinuated that the simple possession of a large number of guns was somehow evidence of crime.

To people who hate firearms, the idea of many dozens of firearms being in the same place is repulsive. Such people have every right to lobby for changes in current firearms law, so as to make it illegal to possess large numbers of firearms without special government permission. But in the absence of such legislation, there is nothing criminal about owning a large number of guns.

While the Branch Davidians did accumulate a huge cache of ammunition, the main reason they seemed to have a large number of guns was because they lived together in the same large building. If the Branch Davidians had, as they did from their founding in 1935 until the late 1980s, lived in separate houses on the same ranch, their gun ownership rate would have been unremarkable by Texas standards. Further, there are many gun collectors in the United States who personally own more firearms than did the Branch Davidians collectively. A large gun collection is entirely lawful and is not evidence of criminal activity.

Obviously, it is not illegal to exercise one's First Amendment rights by believing in a false messiah such as David Koresh. Equally important, to exercise one's Second Amendment rights to the fullest degree is not against the law. Yet the BATF warrant application insinuated that the simple possession of a large number of guns was somehow evidence of crime. Such insinuations are not consistent with a federal agent's oath to uphold the Constitution. For an agency to tolerate such behavior on the part of an agent is a significant sign of the agency's own disregard for the Constitution.

The question for the magistrate was not whether the Branch Davidians were normal and righteous, or weird and sinful, but whether the warrant application presented probable cause to believe that evidence of a crime would be found at the Mount Carmel Center. Under our Constitution, an observation that people are heavily exercising their constitutional rights must not be an element in creating probable cause.

A Flawed Warrant

In evaluating the warrant application and the magistrate's issuance of the warrant, the only facts that are relevant are those presented in the application. If a warrant application presents enough facts to create probable cause, but the resulting search turns up no evidence of a crime, the magistrate should not be criticized. The fact that nothing was found does not retroactively prove that there was not probable cause to search. Conversely, a bad warrant cannot be retroactively validated by the lucky discovery of evidence. Otherwise, there would be no point to the Fourth Amendment's requirement that searches must have a valid warrant based on probable cause.

The BATF affidavit in the warrant application was filled with assertions which were misleading in the extreme. These flaws should not have been present in an affidavit prepared with the aid of two assistant United States attorneys. The federal magistrate's acceptance of the affidavit as the basis for one warrant to arrest Koresh and another warrant to search the entire seventy-seven acre property and the entire house, including the living quarters of over one hundred persons not mentioned in the affidavit, may be partly due to the fact that the warrant application was presented to a relatively inexperienced magistrate. The magistrate, Dennis G. Green, spent much of his legal career as a prosecutor. The Supreme Court requires that the magistrate must "perform his 'neutral and detached' function and not serve merely as a rubber stamp for the police." In a warrant affidavit filled with information irrelevant to the question of whether Koresh and his followers had violated any federal firearms laws, most of the information was misleading regarding the law, guns, gun parts, gun publications, what Koresh and his followers had bought or not bought, and what would or would not constitute a violation of federal laws. . . .

Factual Errors

The legal errors in the affidavit were compounded by much more serious factual errors. Besides asserting knowledge of federal weapons laws, Special Agent Aguilera asserted a knowledge of firearms. He then went on to claim that Koresh had ordered M16 "EZ kits." Aguilera did not note that the kit is called an "E2" kit, not "EZ" (as in "easy" convertibility). The E2 kit is a spare parts kit, not a kit to convert a semi-automatic to full automatic. The E2 kit contains the same spare parts that fit in a semi-automatic Colt AR-15 Sporter or an automatic Colt M16 assault rifle, since the two guns use many common parts.

If the parts from the E2 kit are combined with the receiver from an AR-15 Sporter semi-automatic rifle, the result is a complete AR-15 E2 model semi-automatic rifle. The reason that the E2 kit is not regulated by federal law is that it is not a gun, nor is it a kit designed to convert an ordinary gun to full automatic. Yet the BATF affidavit gave the false impression that the "EZ" kit was made for turning semi-automatic guns into machine guns. Again, none of the spare parts actually alleged to have been delivered to Koresh were conversion kits.

There are two distinct ways of turning an ordinary gun into a machine gun, and Aguilera confused the two. The easy way is to install a conversion kit. As noted above, possession of a conversion kit is subject to the same legal requirements as possession of an actual machine gun. Installation of a conversion kit can be accomplished by anybody who has the patience and dexterity to disassemble a gun down to its very smallest parts (the trigger assembly) and then re-assemble the gun with new parts, according to directions.

The hard way to create a machine gun—the way that must be used by persons without a conversion kit—is to perform extremely high-precision milling and lathing, in order to manufacture the necessary internal components for a machine gun. Aguilera stated accurately that, in unrelated cases, persons have turned semi-automatic AR-15 rifles into machine guns using milling machines and lathes. He also stated accurately that the Branch Davidians had "machinery and implements used or suitable for use in converting semi-automatic weapons to fully automatic weapons and for constructing various destructive devices. . . ." What Aguilera did not tell the magistrate is that hundreds of thousands, perhaps millions, of Americans have access to such basic machine tools in their home workshops or at work. Conversions could be accomplished with an ordinary power drill, if the person doing the conversion were extremely skilled, patient, and careful. . . .

The key evidence [in getting the search and arrest warrants] appears to have been Koresh's religious views, pro-gun rights views, criticism of federal gun laws, and hostility toward the BATF, all of which are protected by the First Amendment.

To suggest that Koresh was intending to convert AR-15 Sporters and semi-automatic imitations of the AK-47 into machine guns, Aguilera's affidavit asserted that Koresh made purchases from a South Carolina company which had all the necessary parts to "convert AR-15 rifles and semi-automatic AK-47 rifles into machine guns if their customers had the upper and lower receivers of those firearms . . . . I know that Howell possesses the upper and lower receivers for the firearms which he is apparently trying to convert to fully automatic." It was highly unlikely, however, that Koresh really did possess "upper and lower receivers" for "semi-automatic AK-47 rifles." Such rifles have a solid block receiver, not separate upper and lower receivers. In any case, Aguilera here was merely hinting that Koresh may have purchased the parts, since there is no allegation that those necessary parts were purchased from the South Carolina firm.

In short, the only evidence that the BATF offered the magistrate that the Davidians were converting semi-automatic guns into machine guns appears to be:

(a) the Davidians had bought the E2 spare parts kit, which BATF falsely claimed was an "EZ" conversion kit;

(b) the Davidians had made unspecified purchases from a company that sells conversion kits, and which also sells thousands of items which are not conversion kits; and

(c) the Davidians owned home workshop equipment such as lathes which can, in addition to many legal uses, be used for illegal fabrication of machine gun components. . . .

In sum, the affidavit insinuated that there was something illegal about the practice of buying a large number of guns and spare parts for those guns, and that there was something illegal about possessing a computer drawing of a machine gun. The evidence of conversion of the legal guns into illegal (unregistered) machine guns was Aguilara's false claims that various spare parts were actually conversion kits.

Liberty magazine summed up the evidence in the warrant application:

> Let us suppose that you and your spouse had a horrible fight, characterized by fervent anger, ugly words and nasty accusations, resulting in your spouse moving out of the home. Let us suppose your spouse goes to the Bureau of Alcohol, Tobacco and Firearms and tells them that you are distilling alcohol without a proper license. The ATF checks with your supermarket and learns that you have over the past few years on numerous occasions purchased sugar and on a few occasions purchased yeast, and verifies with your local utility that you have purchased water. You have acquired all the ingredients needed to manufacture alcohol. The ATF also checks the Treasury's records and verifies that you have never acquired a license to make alcohol.

> In every detail, this situation is identical to the Davidians': there is testimony from an angry former close associate anxious to cause you trouble, there is evidence that you acquired the means to manufacture a product whose manufacture requires a license and there is evidence that you had not obtained the license. Is this ev-

idence—"probable cause"—sufficient for you to lose your right to privacy in your home as guaranteed by the Fourth Amendment?

Actually, the analogy is not quite identical to the Branch Davidian situation. There was no evidence that the Branch Davidians possessed auto sears or conversion kits, which are essential for converting a semiautomatic into an automatic. . . .

False or Irrelevant Accusations

Given the weak state of the evidence against Koresh, the authors of the affidavit bolstered their assertions with a wide variety of accusations which were either patently false or presented in a misleading way.

The affidavit reported that a witness who had been at Mount Carmel in March through June 1992, and was subsequently interviewed by the BATF in January 1993, had "observed at the compound published magazines such as, the *Shotgun News* and other related clandestine magazines." There is nothing remotely clandestine about *Shotgun News*. *Shotgun News* is listed in the *Gale Directory of Publications and Broadcast Media* as being a tri-monthly publication, with a reported circulation of about 165,000. Published by Snell Publishing Company of Hastings, Nebraska, subscriptions are available by mail or telephone; VISA and MasterCard are accepted. The BATF headquarters and various field offices had subscriptions to the "clandestine" publication because the magazine advertises firearms and accessories, as well as many types of other weaponry and collectibles. None of the other alleged "clandestine" publications were identified. . . .

Among the more prominent irrelevant issues in the warrant application are reports involving the abuse of children committed by Koresh. Whether or not the allegations were valid, they did not involve the federal government. However, the investigations of allegations of child abuse by Koresh conducted by the State of Texas are featured in the affidavit of BATF agent Aguilera. The Aguilera affidavit does not mention, however, that the child abuse investigation had been closed for lack of evidence on April 30, 1992, nearly ten months before the assault on Mount Carmel Center.

Another irrelevant and possibly misleading assertion in the affidavit was that a deputy sheriff heard a loud explosion and observed "a large cloud of grey smoke dissipating from ground level." Aguilera was presumably attempting to strengthen the notion that "explosive devices" were possessed by Koresh. The explosion was quite possibly related to the construction of the tornado shelter that the Branch Davidians were building. Aguilera's statement fails to note whether the deputy sheriff who told Aguilera of the explosion also told him if he had investigated the matter and what he had found, or why he had not bothered to investigate.

Other allegations were even weaker, such as a claim by Marc Breault, Koresh's disaffected former lieutenant who had left the residence in 1989, that Koresh had falsely imprisoned a woman in June 1991. The warrant application does not disclose that the FBI had investigated the case in April 1992, and closed the case in June 1992.

After the BATF attack on Mount Carmel, Aguilera returned to court to ask for an expanded search warrant. In the second warrant application, Aguilera reported an incident of child sexual abuse by Koresh which had been alleged by a Texas social worker. No time frame for the alleged abuse was given. Even after the massive shoot-out, Aguilera was apparently still determined to prejudice the courts by bringing up possible violations of Texas state law which, nearly a year before, the State of Texas had found no cause to pursue further.

The September 1993 Treasury Department review offers justification for why BATF—which is not a child welfare agency—kept bringing up stale charges from the child abuse investigation: "While reports that Koresh was permitted to sexually and physically abuse children were not evidence that firearms or explosives violations were occurring, they showed Koresh to have set up a world of his own, where legal prohibitions were disregarded freely." The Treasury Department theory would allow law enforcement agencies to use all allegations of any serious criminal activity to establish probable cause that other crimes were also being committed. . . .

Based on the rambling fifteen-page affidavit by Aguilera which climaxed with the report of agent Rodriguez, Aguilera announced, "I believe that Vernon Howell, also known as David Koresh, and/or his followers . . . are unlawfully manufacturing and possessing machineguns and explosive devices."

Magistrate Green apparently agreed, and on February

25, 1993, issued a search warrant for machine guns and destructive devices and an arrest warrant for Vernon Howell, a.k.a. David Koresh, for possession of destructive devices. The key evidence appears to have been Koresh's religious views, pro-gun rights views, criticism of federal gun laws, and hostility toward the BATF, all of which are protected by the First Amendment. . . .

The Waco warrant application was deeply flawed, and riddled with misleading or false statements of law and fact. The warrant application illustrates the low standards to which some federal law enforcement agencies, and United States Attorney's offices, have declined as a result of lax attitudes towards warrants in too much of the judiciary, including a majority of the United States Supreme Court. As a remedy, Congress should enact legislation restoring search and seizure standards to full strength.

3

The FBI Deserves Praise, Not Blame

Edward S.G. Dennis Jr.

When the Waco standoff ended, Edward S.G. Dennis Jr. was appointed to evaluate the strategy and tactics used by the U.S. Department of Justice and the Federal Bureau of Investigation during the standoff. In the excerpts from his report printed below, Dennis offers an overview of the FBI approach, and notes that there were some strategic disagreements between the bureau's negotiators and the tactical team. Nonetheless, he defends the FBI strategy. It is not the case, he insists, that FBI negotiators failed to take seriously Koresh's religious framework during their discussions with him. According to Dennis, Koresh's theology was peculiar enough that he was beyond the reach of religious scholars who may have sought to reason with him over his biblical interpretations. Furthermore, Dennis says, the FBI made judicious use of behavioral experts in planning its strategy. Finally, he concludes, although FBI performance could have been improved in some areas, the blame for the breakdown in negotiations rests squarely on Koresh rather than on the bureau. As he sees it, the fifty-one-day standoff was a "mass suicide choreographed by Koresh" during which "the FBI exhibited extraordinary restraint." Dennis was acting deputy attorney general of the United States in 1989 and has been a senior partner in the law firm of Morgan, Lewis, and Bockius since 1990.

T he first briefing book presented to the Attorney General states that the strategy was to "secure the surren-

Edward S.G. Dennis Jr., "Evaluation of the Handling of the Branch Davidian Stand-Off in Waco, Texas, February 28 to April 19, 1993," www.usdoj.gov, U.S. Department of Justice, October 8, 1993.

der and arrest of all adult occupants of the compound while providing the maximum possible security for the children within the compound." The negotiators knew they were faced with a religious group fanatically devoted to [David] Koresh and his teachings. It was not certain, however, whether Koresh truly believed his own religious message or whether he was exploiting his control over his followers for personal gain.

Initially the FBI tried to work within the framework of the Davidians' beliefs to convince Koresh the standoff was not the apocalyptic event he had prophesied. Evidently Koresh was the only "expert" in his branch of Branch Davidianism, and so even with advice from religious scholars, the FBI was unable to influence Koresh's unique interpretation of scripture. The frustration of working within Koresh's religious framework became apparent when on March 2, 1993, after promising to leave the compound, Koresh said that God had told him to wait. Koresh was improvising his own theology and was completely beyond the influence of religious arguments or religious scholars.

Koresh could not be pressured into leaving the compound, and whatever bound Koresh and his followers was apparently stronger than either force or reason.

Koresh knew that he and other Davidians would be arrested and charged with murder of the ATF [Alcohol, Tobacco & Firearms] agents. Koresh and others in the compound were acutely aware of the secular consequences of their acts. Texas has the death penalty by lethal injection. At one point in the negotiations Koresh joked, "When they give me the lethal injection, give me the cheap stuff, huh?" Efforts were aimed at convincing Koresh that if he and the others exited the compound they would be treated well and that they might "beat the rap." Needless to say this tactic was not popular since it implicitly criticized ATF and could be viewed as disparaging of the four dead ATF agents. However, the tactic was completely proper in the context of negotiating a nonviolent end to the standoff.

In the face of Koresh's intransigence the final negotiating strategy was developed called the "trickle, flow, gush" strategy. The objective was to undermine the devotion of individual members to Koresh. The FBI began speaking to the other members on the phone, playing tapes of the negotiations and the statements of released members and family members back into the compound over loud speakers, sending videotapes and pictures of the released children into the compound and sending in messages from family members. For example, a taped passage from the negotiations in which Special Agent Byron Sage outwitted Koresh was played over the loudspeakers for this purpose. The objective was to move the pace of the exodus from the compound from a trickle to a flow to a mass desertion of Koresh by his followers.

Although others left the compound, this strategy also failed. The number of people leaving the compound slowed rather than accelerated and the exit of members from the compound stopped altogether after March 23rd, nearly a month before the final assault. There is evidence that Koresh was purging his group and therefore these departures from the compound did not represent defections from Koresh's ranks. Many of the adults leaving the compound appeared to remain loyal to Koresh.

Koresh broke his promises to leave the compound, and the pace of the releases did not significantly increase. Koresh had promised to come out on March 2nd if the government played his tape. The government complied and Koresh reneged. Koresh said he was waiting for a sign from God. On March 12 he considered the guitar nebula as a possible sign, but decided it was not the sign he was waiting for. Koresh told his lawyers he would come out after Passover, but when Passover ended, Koresh said he had not committed to a specific date to come out. Koresh continued to make excuses to stay in the compound thus reinforcing the view that he was not devout, only manipulative.

Dr. Park Dietz, a Clinical Professor of Psychiatry and Behavioral Sciences at the University of California, was consulted by the FBI. Dr. Dietz is under contract with the FBI as a forensic psychiatrist. The FBI flew Dr. Dietz to Mt. Carmel to give his assessment of Koresh. March 2nd Dr. Dietz expressed the opinion that Koresh would not voluntarily leave the compound. He considered Koresh to be suicidal and stated that Koresh might have made a suicide pact with his followers. Dr. Dietz described Koresh's personality as manipulative.

Dr. Dietz made a number of recommendations based on his review of documents and the negotiations up to that point. He recommended that the FBI distance itself from ATF and express sympathy with Koresh's anti-BATF views. Dr. Dietz expressed the opinion that Koresh would choose death over losing power, and therefore the negotiation strategy should create the illusion that Koresh would not go to prison but would emerge with more followers than he had before.

Some negotiators believe that as a result of these actions the Davidians concluded that the negotiators had no influence over the decision makers and that the FBI was not trustworthy. Several negotiators and behavioral scientists expressed the opinion that although David Koresh and his core followers may never have come out through negotiation, more people might have exited the compound voluntarily during the standoff if the negotiation strategy had been followed more rigorously.

The negotiators recognized that a traditional negotiation tactic is to put pressure on the subject at times through tactical activities choreographed with a more gentle negotiating approach. However, a memorandum dated March 5, 1993, from FBI behavioral scientists stated that "[i]n traditional hostage situations, a strategy which has been successful has been negotiations coupled with ever increasing tactical presence. In this situation however, it is believed this strategy, if carried to excess, could eventually be counter productive and could result in loss of life."

Total Allegiance

Despite these conflicts, I am not confident that more members would have left the compound if the negotiating strategy had been followed more rigorously. Even though in hindsight the behavioral assessment of Koresh proved extremely accurate, the most compelling evidence of the resolve of the Davidians to follow Koresh was their willingness to take their own lives and the lives of their children in obedience to Koresh. It is this total allegiance to Koresh that was unpredictable. Even those who left the compound before the fire seemed to remain committed to him. Several expressed regret that they could not join him in death. Koresh could not be pressured into leaving the compound, and whatever bound Koresh and his followers was apparently stronger than either force or reason. . . .

Tension Within the FBI

Conflicts were reported between the negotiators and the tactical elements regarding the strategy to be used with the Davidians. On several occasions tactical pressure was exerted on the Davidians either without consulting the negotiators or over the negotiators' objections. The negotiators believed the timing of these tactical activities disrupted the progress of the negotiations unnecessarily. Additionally, negotiators complained that the HRT [Hostage Rescue Team] engaged in tactical maneuvers before the negotiators had an opportunity to use the maneuvers to further the bargaining process.

At the outset of the crisis FBI behavioral scientists recommended against confronting David Koresh. The negotiators specifically recommended that the Bradley [armored] vehicles should not be brought up to the compound. Despite the negotiators' advice, the Bradleys were run up and down in front of the compound in what negotiators believed was a show of force.

On March 12 after two Davidians had exited the compound the decision was made to turn off the electricity in the compound. The negotiators objected to the decision arguing that the Davidians should be rewarded for releasing two people. The power was turned off. No one was released for the next seven days.

On March 21 after seven Davidians had exited the compound the negotiators were advised that the Davidian vehicles would be cleared from the left side of the compound. The negotiators opposed this action, pointing out that once again the FBI would be answering a positive move on the part of the Branch Davidians by a negative action. Nonetheless, the bulldozing was implemented. The negotiators received conflicting justifications for the action, being told both that the items were being moved as a safety measure and to harass the Davidians.

Loudspeakers were initially used to provide information to Koresh's followers still inside the compound, but contrary to the negotiators' advice the loudspeakers were used to broadcast Tibetan chants, other annoying music and the sounds of dying rabbits. The negotiators objected to playing music as a harassment tactic, advising that such "psychological warfare" would only make the FBI look bad.

For the standoff in Waco the FBI called upon the services of the Criminal Investigative Analysis subunit, which falls under the Investigative Support Unit of the FBI's NCAVC [National Center for the Analysis of Violent Crime]. The special agents in this subunit offer assistance such as personality assessments of known individuals, suggestions as to strategy and on-site assistance with major violent crimes.

In addition to FBI experts, outside experts were consulted by the FBI during the Waco standoff. These experts specialized in the fields of psychology and psychiatry and provided behavioral assessments of Koresh and his followers. Park Elliot Dietz, Clinical Professor of Psychiatry and Biobehavioral Sciences from the University of California School of Medicine and a civilian consultant to the FBI, provided assistance evaluating Koresh. Bruce D. Perry, Chief of Psychiatry of the Baylor College, worked with the released children and provided some assessments of Koresh's likely actions based on that work. Psychiatrist Joseph Krofcheck and psycholinguist Murray Miron assisted in analyzing Koresh's letters which were sent out at the end of the standoff.

The behavioral experts were provided access to all of the material gathered by the ATF regarding Koresh and the Davidians, including interviews of former members and records of prior criminal proceedings. In addition the behavioral scientists listened to the ongoing negotiations and spoke with those who interviewed the released children. The behavioral scientists expressed no dissatisfaction with the quantity and quality of information with which they were presented. Indeed, one of them remarked that even though the ATF had not gathered this information for the purposes of creating a psychological profile, they had all the information that was necessary.

Behavioral Scientists Assess Koresh

The chronology of the written advice from the behavioral scientists is as follows: on March 3, 1993 the behavioral experts wrote a joint memo recommending a strategy of trying to work within the Davidians' own belief system to talk them out. They recommended acknowledging the conspiracy against the Davidians and their right to defend themselves, and creating an illusion that Koresh could win in court and in the press and would not go to jail. On March 5 behavioral experts wrote a memo advising that the negotiation strategy focus on insuring the safety of the children and facilitating the peaceful surrender of the Davidians. This memo recommended a de-escalation of tactical pressure because movement of tactical personnel would validate Koresh's prophesy that his followers must die defending their faith. As an alternative tactic, the memo recommends that efforts be made to drive a wedge between Koresh and his followers by convincing them that a battle is not inevitable.

It appears that the behavioral scientists did not simply apply a one-dimensional diagnosis of anti-social personality, but took seriously the possibility that Koresh was also a delusional person willing to die and see his followers die according to his teachings.

They recommended continuing efforts to establish a wedge between Koresh and his followers using outside family members and released children to appeal to the parents, gaining direct intelligence about activities inside the compound and giving Koresh's followers the opportunity to safely break and run.

A memo of March 7, 1993, lists certain tactical activities that might be used to "increase the stress and anxiety" inside the compound, including many of the things that ultimately were done, such as floodlights, noises, loudspeakers, movement of military vehicles, shutting off utilities, fencing off the compound and discrediting Koresh at press conferences. However, the memo also cautions against tactical options which would shut down the negotiations, because then the only option would be physical action with the Davidians fighting to the death and tremendous loss of life. The memo recommended continued negotiation with the use of Sheriff Harwell [the local sheriff, whom Koresh knew] as a third party intermediary.

A March 8, 1993, memo sets forth a psychological profile of Koresh. The memo points out that Koresh shows signs of being a religious fanatic with delusions. The memo speculates that Koresh may have ambushed the ATF agents on February 28 "to set into motion a chain of events which will verify, to his followers, that his interpretation of the scriptures . . . is correct." The memo acknowledges that "[i]t has been speculated that Koresh's religious beliefs are nothing more than a con, in order to get power, money, women, etc., and that a strong show of force (tanks, [Armored Personnel Carriers], weapons, etc.) will crumble that resolve, causing him to surrender." In fact, the memo warns, the opposite may well occur and Koresh and his followers will draw closer together. The March 8 memo also recognizes that "[t]he strong show of force response is to be expected from law enforcement personnel, who are action oriented," but that Koresh may be trying to provoke a confrontation where the FBI unintentionally makes his prophecy come true. The memo warns that Koresh's teachings have been that his followers must follow him in death, even if that means killing themselves and that Koresh might order a mass suicide rather than lose his status as Messiah. The memo advises doing the opposite of what one would do in traditional hostage negotiations with a psychopath (i.e. wresting control), but rather moving back would be taking power from Koresh. It concludes "[t]he bottom line is that we can always resort to tactical pressure, but it should be the absolute last option."

A memo dated March 9, 1993, recommends that efforts should be made to break Koresh's spirit because his psychopathic tendencies to control and manipulate have caused the negotiations to meet with limited success. The memo recommends "nonoffensive" actions, such as sporadic termination and reinstating of utilities, unpredictable movement of manpower and equipment, downplaying Koresh in press conferences, jamming radio and television and denying negotiations to demonstrate that Koresh is no longer in charge and to buy time. A March 7 memo from headquarters suggests that small failures will cause the followers to question Koresh. At this point the behavioral science memos ceased.

A Diagnosis of Mental Illness

On April 9 and 10 Koresh sent out two letters which were analyzed by psycholinguist Murray S. Miron and psychiatrist Joseph Krofcheck, working with FBI agent Clinton Van Zandt. Miron assessed Koresh from the first letter as exhibiting a "rampant, morbidly virulent paranoia" and "dissociative pathology which makes him oblivious to either reality or rationality." Miron sees the letter as a "delusional communication" implying that Koresh is preparing to do battle against his adversaries, that he is in a mindset of aggressiveness and may have provided for "snares" against an assault on the compound. Krofcheck analyzes the same letter as showing Koresh to be a "functional, paranoid type personality" and a "charismatic, manipulative person with a core delusional system that sees himself as his own form of the trinity consisting of God, Jesus Christ and David Koresh, the prophet through whom God speaks." He believes Koresh is exercising self-deception and that he has no real intention to comply with any demands. Koresh is seen as a user of others who does not value his people as equals or human beings. He plans to catch the FBI unaware, which could include destruction by fire or explosion. "He may be prepared to do whatever he has to do to fulfill his ultimate game plan." "He is willing to kill, to see his followers die and to die himself." "Koresh's clock is running and he is fully capable of creating the circumstances to bring this matter to a 'magnificent' end in his mind, a conclusion that could take the lives of all of his followers and as many of the authorities as possible." Krofcheck believes Koresh will not come out voluntarily and "the government is the hostage." Krofcheck concludes that "we have no clear ability to influence the exit of him and his followers from their compound short of tactical intervention."

Finally, on April 17, just before the final assault plan was approved, Park Dietz was asked to give his views on the status of the negotiations and prognosis for a successful conclusion. In a memo dated April 17 Dietz opined that negotiating in good faith would not resolve the situation as it now stands. However, he believed the negotiations did not succeed because of the ATF's continued involvement in the case and the fact that negotiation strategies were "repeatedly undermined by ancillary actions." Dietz stated that Koresh would not come out or send out substantial numbers of his followers and that conditions inside the compound would continue to deteriorate.

From these memos it appears that the behavioral scientists did not simply apply a one-dimensional diagnosis of anti-social personality, but took seriously the possibility that Koresh was also a delusional person willing to die and see his followers die according to his teachings. . . .

The Davidians were given every opportunity to leave the compound. Ultimately, under Koresh's total control, some or all of them chose to kill themselves, to kill each other and to murder their own children, rather than to surrender to law enforcement authorities and face the consequences of their armed resistance of the ATF. In the final analysis the deaths of the Davidians were caused by David Koresh. . . .

Praising the FBI

David Koresh engaged in a deliberate campaign to mask his true intentions. Even so, the FBI was extremely accurate in its assessment of Koresh. I conclude that the standoff was a mass suicide choreographed by Koresh over a two month period. Even if the FBI had been more keenly aware of his intentions, it was limited to gassing the compound as the only non-lethal means of resolving the crisis. The probability that the FBI could have broken Koresh's hold over his followers through negotiations was extremely low based upon what we have learned following the incident.

Under the circumstances, the FBI exhibited extraordinary restraint and handled this crisis with great professionalism.

4

The FBI Strategy Did Not Take Religious Beliefs Seriously

James D. Tabor

In the following selection, James D. Tabor argues that the FBI's strategy at Waco was deeply flawed. According to Tabor, a religious studies professor at the University of North Carolina at Charlotte, the FBI was woefully ignorant of the biblical scriptures that were of central concern to Koresh and the rest of the Branch Davidians. He recounts how he quickly came to believe that negotiators would have to be able to discuss biblical issues knowledgeably and seriously in order to achieve a peaceful resolution to the standoff, and hence he offered his services to the FBI. According to Tabor, Koresh believed that the situation he and other members of the Branch Davidians were in was one predicted by the Book of Revelation, and thus, Tabor says, Koresh made decisions about what to do next in accordance with his interpretation of that part of the Bible. Tabor argues that he and a colleague, Phillip Arnold, were successful in persuading Koresh of a different interpretation of the Book of Revelation, one in which God wanted Koresh to write down his views on certain religious issues and then surrender to the authorities. Tabor says that Koresh was in the middle of this project when the FBI stormed the residence, and that he is certain Koresh would have surrendered as soon as he finished the work.

It was 7:25 P.M. on Sunday, February 28, 1993. My attention was suddenly riveted to an unfamiliar voice, edged

James D. Tabor, "The Waco Tragedy: An Autobiographical Account of One Attempt to Avert Disaster," *From the Ashes: Making Sense of Waco*, edited by James R. Lewis. Lanham, MD: Rowman and Littlefield, 1993. Copyright © 1993 by Rowman and Littlefield. Reproduced by permission.

with an appealing intensity, coming over CNN on the television in the next room. Anchorman David French had someone on a phone hookup who was quoting biblical passages in a steady stream. A photo of a young man with glasses and long wavy hair, which was later to become familiar around the world, was on the TV screen against a backdrop of a map of Texas with a place marked as "Mt. Carmel," near Waco. Regular CNN programming had been interrupted. It was obvious that some emergency situation was unfolding. I had not yet heard of the Alcohol, Tobacco, and Firearms Bureau raid on Mt. Carmel that very morning at 9:55 A.M. which resulted in a two-hour gun battle with Branch Davidians, the religious group which lived there, leaving four ATF agents dead and fifteen wounded. For the moment my attention was drawn to two things which fascinated me. The young man from Texas called himself David Koresh, and he was talking about the "seven seals" of the Book of Revelation. As a biblical scholar I knew that Koresh was the Hebrew word for Cyrus, the ancient Persian king who destroyed the Babylonian empire in 539 B.C.E. I was intrigued that anyone would have such a last name. Also, I was quite familiar with the mysterious seven seals in the last book of the Bible, and how they unfolded in an apocalyptic sequence leading to the Judgment Day and the "end of the world." Like any good newsperson, CNN anchorman French kept trying to get David Koresh to talk about the morning raid, how many had been killed or wounded from his group, and whether he planned to surrender. Koresh admitted he was wounded badly, that his two-year-old daughter had been killed, and some others were killed and wounded from his group. But it was clear that he mainly wanted to quote scriptures, mostly from the Book of Revelation. He said he was the Lamb, chosen to open the Seven Seals. He challenged religious leaders and biblical scholars from around the world to come to Texas and engage in debate with him on the Bible, and particularly to try and match his understanding in unlocking the mystery of the Seven Seals.

The phone conversation over CNN went on for about forty-five minutes. I was utterly taken with this whole scene. Here we were in the year 1993 and this young Cyrus, would-be challenger of modern Babylon, was actually delving into the details of the Book of Revelation at prime time, over a worldwide television network. . . .

The FBI Steps In

Over the next few days, as the FBI took over control of the siege of the Mt. Carmel complex, it became clear to me that neither the officials in charge, nor the media who were sensationally reporting the sexual escapades of David Koresh, had a clue about the *biblical* world which this group inhabited. Their entire frame of reference came from the Bible, especially from the Book of Revelation and the ancient Hebrew prophets. I realized that in order to deal with David Koresh, and to have any chance for a peaceful resolution of the Waco situation, one would have to understand and make use of these biblical texts. In other words, one would need to enter into the apocalyptic world of David Koresh and his dedicated followers. It was obvious that they were willing to die for what they believed, and they would not surrender under threat of force. I decided to contact the FBI and offer my services.

As the FBI took over control of the siege . . . it became clear to me that neither the officials in charge, nor the media . . . had a clue about the biblical *world which this group inhabited.*

I called my friend Phillip Arnold, director of Reunion Institute in Houston, Texas. Dr. Arnold, like me, is a specialist in biblical studies and we share a special interest in both ancient and modern forms of *apocalypticism*. The term comes from the Greek word *apocalypsis*, which means "to uncover, to reveal." The Book of Revelation is often called the Apocalypse. An apocalyptic group is one which believes that the end of history is near and that the signs and secrets of the final scenario have been revealed to them. The followers of Jesus are properly understood as an apocalyptic movement within ancient Judaism, as was the group which produced the Dead Sea Scrolls. Since the third century B.C.E. many such groups, first Jewish and later Christian, have proclaimed the imminent end of the world on the basis of their understanding of biblical prophetic texts. Dr. Arnold agreed with me that it was urgent and vital that someone who understood the biblical texts become involved in the situation.

The first FBI agent Dr. Arnold contacted in Waco admitted that they were hopelessly confused when David Koresh went into one of his lengthy expositions of scripture, which occurred regularly in their daily telephone negotiations. In later interviews with survivors of the Waco tragedy the one point that they made repeatedly and consistently was that the source of their attraction to David Koresh was his knowledge of the scriptures, particularly the Book of Revelation. The FBI does not routinely pack Bibles when facing what they had categorized as a hostage situation. This FBI agent told us how they had been frantically reading through the Book of Revelation in the Gideon Bibles in their hotel rooms. This image struck me as almost comical, but at the same time frightening. The agent also told us they found the Book of Revelation, and David Koresh's extended biblical monologues, wholly incomprehensible. . . .

A Different Approach

Over the next few weeks Dr. Arnold and I spent many hours in technical and lengthy discussions with Livingston Fagan, an articulate member of the Branch Davidians who had been sent out of the compound by David Koresh as a spokesperson and was being held in jail. With our knowledge of the prophetic texts of the Bible, and especially the Book of Revelation, we slowly began to attain some understanding of David Koresh's interpretation.

It became obvious to us that the Branch Davidian group understood itself to be actually living through the events of the seven seals, found primarily in chapter six of the Book of Revelation. We became persuaded that they understood themselves to be "in the fifth seal. . . ."

We discussed the chilling implications of these verses [Rev 6: 9–11, which discuss the fifth seal] with the FBI. For the Koresh group the Book of Revelation was like a script, setting forth in vivid detail what would transpire, and instructing them as to what they should do. The reason they refused to come out of their compound was that they felt God was telling them in these verses to wait "a little season." But the verse goes on to predict that they, like the others in the February 28 ATF raid, would then be killed. David Koresh once told the federal agents, "I knew you were coming before you knew you were coming." On the morning of that initial raid David had said to ATF undercover agent Robert Rodriguez, who was spying on the group, "What thou doest, do quickly" (John 13:27). David had been studying the Bible with agent Rodriguez for weeks, even though he had figured out he was working for the ATF, and now considered him a Judas figure, who had been given an opportunity to know the truth but rejected it. It was as if the entire situation in Waco was locked into a predetermined pattern, set forth in a book written around 96 C.E., during the reign of the Roman emperor Domitian. What worried us all was the very real possibility of a self-fulfilling prophecy. If the Koresh group found itself living "in the fifth seal," did that mean it was inevitable that the remaining eighty-seven men, women, and children in the Mt. Carmel compound must also die? Might they not provoke a violent end to things simply because they felt it was the predetermined will of God, moving things along to the sixth seal, which was the great Judgment Day of God? We were fascinated by the way in which the literal words of this text dominated the entire situation. David Koresh insisted to the FBI that God had told him to "wait" an unspecified time, and the FBI constantly pushed him, asking, "How long?" The entire drama was being played out according to a biblical script.

Talking to Koresh

Through hours of conversations with one another, and consultation with Livingston Fagan, we slowly began to map out the apocalyptic scenario or "script" that David Koresh and his followers were expecting. We were absolutely convinced that David would never surrender from pressure or harassment. Given his understanding of himself as the messenger, or "anointed one," who had been given the secret of the seven seals, he would only act as he felt God was leading him. And the text of the Book of Revelation was his primary guide. According to his reading of the seven seals, five had now been fulfilled and God was telling him to wait. Given such a view, he simply would not come out and surrender as the FBI demanded. To Koresh and his followers such a move, before the proper time, would have been inconceivable. They would have seen it as disobedience to God. Slowly we formulated a plan to approach David Koresh with an alternative scenario, seeking to meet him within his own interpretive world.

Our first step was a radio broadcast over KGBS, the Dallas radio station which Koresh and his followers tuned to each morning on their battery operated transistor radios. It was April 1, thirty-three days since the siege had begun. The talk show host, Ron Engelman, who had been critical of the federal authorities since the February 28 ATF raid, allowed us full use of air time to begin a dialogue with Koresh. Dick DeGuerin, Koresh's attorney who had been meeting with him for the past four days, was clued into our plan. He assured us that Koresh and his followers would be listening to our discussion. What we presented, in give-and-take dialogue form, was a rather technical discussion of an alternative interpretation of the Book of Revelation, which we thought David Koresh might accept. As academics, we were not presenting this interpretation as our own personal view. Rather, our approach was hypothetical—given Koresh's general world view, and the interpretation he was following of the seven seals, what about an alternative understanding? Three days later, on Sunday, April 4th, Dick DeGuerin also took a cassette tape we had made of our discussion of the Book of Revelation into the Mt. Carmel compound so that David Koresh and his followers would have it to listen to and study. Passover was approaching, an eight-day holiday which the Branch Davidians observed. Koresh had announced that following the Passover festival he would announce his plan for surrender.

Koresh Pledges to Come Out

On Wednesday, April 14th, just five days before the fire that consumed the compound, David Koresh released a letter through his lawyer. It was to be his last. He said that at long last his wait was over; that he had been instructed by God to write an exposition expounding the secrets of the seven seals of Revelation. He wrote:

> I am presently being permitted to document in structured form the decoded messages of the seven seals. Upon the completion of this task, I will be freed of my waiting period. I hope to finish this as soon as possible and stand before man and answer any and all questions regarding my activities. . . . I have been praying for so long for this opportunity to put the Seals in written form. Speaking the truth seems to have very little effect

on man. I have been shown that as soon as I am given over to the hands of man, I will be made a spectacle of and people will not be concerned about the truth of God, but just the bizarrity of me in the flesh. I want the people of this generation to be saved. I am working night and day to complete my final work of writing out these seals. I thank my Father, He has finally granted me this chance to do this. It will bring new light and hope for many and they won't have to deal with me the person. As soon as I can see that people like Jim Tabor and Phil Arnold have a copy, I will come out and then you can do your thing with this beast. . . .

There is not the slightest doubt in my mind that David Koresh would have surrendered peacefully when he finished his manuscript. After the fire some federal agents said they doubted that he was even working on such a project. They took David's talk about being allowed by God to finally write the interpretation of the seven seals as a ploy to further delay things. We now know this was not the case. Ruth Riddle, one of the survivors of the fire, had a computer disk in the right pocket of her jacket. She had been typing David's hand-written manuscript the day before the fire. On that disk was his exposition of the first seal. The disk is in the possession of the federal authorities.

5

The Decision to Use CS Gas Was Justified

Janet Reno

In the following piece, Janet Reno, at the time the attorney general of the United States, defends the decision to use CS gas in an effort to compel Koresh and the other Branch Davidians to surrender. Speaking in 1995 to a special Capitol Hill committee investigating the federal government's handling of the standoff, Reno argues that the gas was used as a last resort, after extended negotiation had failed. According to Reno, Koresh's promise to surrender was merely a delaying tactic, and she insists that there was an urgent need to bring the standoff to an end. Furthermore, she says, CS gas is the best understood and safest tear gas in the world, and its introduction on April 19, 1993, was done slowly and with great care.

Three days after the Waco standoff began, David Koresh promised the FBI that he and his followers would surrender immediately after a tape he had made was broadcast on the radio. The tape was broadcast. What did he do? He broke his word. He did not surrender. In fact, while the tape was being broadcast, Koresh and his followers were not gathering their belongings and preparing to surrender peacefully. Instead, they were busy rehearsing a plan to blow themselves up and take as many agents as possible with them by walking out of the compound with explosives strapped to their waists.

On March 19 and 20, Koresh said he would come out

Janet Reno, "Capitol Hill Hearing: Joint Hearing of the Crime Subcommittee of the House Judiciary Committee and the National Security International Affairs and Criminal Justice Subcommittee of the House Government Reform and Oversight Committee; Review of Siege of Branch Davidians' Compound in Waco, Texas," *Federal News Service*, August 1, 1995.

soon. He did not. In early April, he said he would come out after Passover. He did not. On April the 14th, he let his lawyers believe he needed only a few days to complete his manuscript on the seven seals, and he would then surrender. The FBI showed Koresh's April 14 letter to an expert at Syracuse University, who concluded it was another ploy, another delaying tactic.

But the FBI kept negotiating. They kept asking Koresh when he would finish the seven seals and come out. On April the 15th, the negotiators asked Steve Schneider, Koresh's second in command, whether he had seen any finished pages of the manuscript. Schneider said he had not. On April the 16th, the negotiators asked Steven Schneider again whether Koresh had completed the first seal. Schneider said no. On the 17th, Schneider said he couldn't say whether it would be six months or six years.

It's easy, in hindsight, to suggest the so-called surrender offer of April 14 was a missed opportunity, but we considered it carefully. We didn't dismiss it casually. Even though Koresh broke every promise he made and even though he never gave the FBI any reason to believe he would surrender peacefully, the FBI kept negotiating, kept trying every way they knew how to talk Koresh into leaving, but he never gave them a specific date.

A Need for Action

When I took office on March the 12th, 1993, the most urgent issue I faced was how to bring the standoff to a safe and peaceful end. Remember why we were in Waco: Four federal agents had been killed trying to arrest Koresh and to seize illegal explosives and illegal weapons, including hand grenades, grenade launchers, and machine guns. We couldn't just walk away from it.

Day after day, FBI negotiators tried to arrange a surrender. During the standoff, the FBI had 949 conversations with Koresh or his lieutenants, totalling almost 215 hours. At the urging of the FBI, the local sheriff attempted to get Koresh to surrender. So did several lawyers and others who were given extraordinary access to the compound.

We faced an impossible situation. Koresh wouldn't leave. He had told the FBI as early as March 7 that no more children would be released. What to do next? We studied intelligence reports. We met with outside experts. The perimeter was becoming increasingly unstable, with frequent reports of outsiders, including at least one militia group, on the way either to help Koresh or attack him. The FBI's hostage rescue team was nearing its seventh week at Waco, and experts had advised me that they would soon have to be pulled back for retraining if they were to maintain their state of readiness.

We checked on the Davidians' food and water supplies, and I was advised that they had provisions to last up to a year. I asked the FBI to check the water supply again, and I was advised the supply was plentiful and it was constantly being replenished.

Clearly, a dangerous situation was becoming more dangerous, especially for the children. We had received allegations that Koresh had sexually abused the children in the past, including Kiri Jewell when she was just 10 years old. We had also received allegations that Koresh had physically abused the children. For example, a former Davidian alleged that Koresh had once spanked a young child for 40 minutes so hard that her bottom was bleeding. The child was only eight months old.

During the standoff, the environment in which Koresh forced those children to remain continued to deteriorate. Human waste was being dumped into the courtyard.

The FBI submitted a plan to use an irritant gas incrementally, beginning at one end of the compound, to shrink the usable space, to induce Koresh to start letting his people go. I asked whether the gas could cause permanent harm, especially to the children and the elderly. Dr. Harry Salem told me, as he told you again last week, that CS gas was the safest, best-studied tear gas in the world. He told me the gas would not cause any permanent harm to the children and the elderly.

Careful and Patient

The April 19 operation began with clear announcements of our intentions, repeated time and time again, aimed at giving the Branch Davidians opportunities to leave safely. The Davidians responded with heavy gunfire from the tower and other parts of the compound.

Yes, we had hoped the Davidians might not react violently if we used the gas in a slow, incremental manner, but those hopes were dashed by the Davidians and their guns. Our response was measured. We inserted gas, then waited, then inserted more gas. We were very careful never to insert more gas than a fraction of the safe limit.

Six hours went by, six hours, and still no one came out. The rest you know. The Branch Davidians were recorded while they spread the fuels used to ignite the fire that resulted in the deaths of all but nine. FBI agents risked their lives to rescue several of them. Others emerged through holes the tanks had made in the walls after it was learned that other exits had been blocked from the inside.

I asked whether the gas could cause permanent harm, especially to the children and the elderly. Dr. Harry Salem told me, as he told you again last week, that CS gas was the safest, best-studied tear gas in the world.

We will never know whether there was a better solution. Had we not acted when we did, and Koresh had brought things to a sudden and violent finish as he had rehearsed, we would probably be here today anyhow. And you would be asking me why I hadn't taken action earlier; why we had not tried to use tear gas to resolve the situation. Everyone involved in the events of April the 19th made their best judgments based on all the information we had. We have tried as hard as we can to study what happened at Waco, to learn from our experience and to make changes so that as we go forward, we can be as prepared as possible to deal with such future situations. . . .

[Rep. Steven Schiff]: Madam Attorney General, having recognized that you got into a very difficult, inherently difficult situation, as has been stated, I think there are some legitimate questions that we might ask you about. One is, you stated that your first concern was about the effects of CS gas that were used. I think that's an understandable concern. I asked all of the witnesses who testified as experts about CS gas, did they know any precedent anywhere in the world where there was a plan to pump CS gas into a building for 48 hours straight, which was part of the FBI's plan, and they all answered no.

And I asked the witnesses, did they know of any precedent anywhere in the world for the deliberate insertion of

CS gas into a building for any length of time in which there were children, and particularly infants, present, and they said no. And I'm wondering if, when you were being advised about CS gas, if you asked that question about "Has this been done before as the FBI wishes to do it in this case?"

Reno: We explored it because I was trying to see whether there were other circumstances. I don't think that I learned of any other circumstances in which a similar situation was involved. And so I don't think that we were able to find any precedent for it.

Rep. Schiff: Wouldn't that kind of indicate that there could be a problem with that plan if you can't find any precedent for it?

Reno: One of the points that we tried to address was, did we have any record of it? Did we know anything? We went to everything that we could find. I consulted with Dr. Salem. He consulted with or talked to a pediatrician, as I understand it, trying to see what we knew, coming to the point that, considering everything, considering the fact that they had rehearsed a plan to come out with explosives on them, blow themselves and agents up and others commit suicide, how could we best control it, under what circumstances.

And taking everything into consideration, I made the best judgment I could based on the information that we had available and with the understanding—because I've gone back and double checked this. One of the things that I want to try to do is to make sure that if new information is developed, we pursue it to see how we can learn from what we have done to avoid a problem for the future. We brought in the British experts to make sure that we had outside judgments to see, to look, to explore, and they confirmed that the amount of gas, as I understand it, coming into the compound during that six to seven hours, was more than within safe limits. . . .

Rep. Robert Ehrlich: Madam Attorney General, we appreciate your being here today. I have a couple of very specific questions. You understand time is short; I'm going to ask them pretty quickly here. With respect to the element of child abuse, I'm firmly convinced that gross abuses of children occurred in that compound prior to the first raid. My question to you though is, specifically after the initial attack, during the siege, were you relying on any firm pieces of evidence regarding continuation of child abuse by Koresh against those kids? And if the answer's yes, did that play—was that element in your ultimate decision to proceed with the raid, the second raid?

Reno: The factor of child abuse was—because we had clear information that there had been allegations of child abuse that had occurred before the raid, and I heard and understood during the course of the briefing that he was beating the children at the time. I asked, is he beating the children? And going back over it with the FBI, what they had understood was that we had evidence of those that had come out; that there had been beatings, and they expected that they were continuing. What prompted me, for example, Dr. Perry testifying before you said that two of the children who had come out after the raid had physical lesions on them from the beatings that they had received. And so it was this continuing feature, and the fact that he had sexually abused the children according to the best information we could gather; that there was evidence of this physical beating, that was clearly one of the factors I considered.

Those children, no matter how they were found, the fact that they are dead is a tragedy that will be with me for the rest of my life.

Rep. Ehrlich: Alright that's the answer to my question. Also, did the element of sexual child abuse enter into it as well?

Reno: Yes. . . .

Rep. John Mica: Your plan was to continue pumping CS gas into Mount Carmel and you—the question I have is, were you aware, again, with infants and children, almost two dozen of them, that one of the major errors in this is that they didn't have the ability to protect themselves from this gas? Were you aware that the gas masks that they had actually couldn't fit on women and children? This is a copy of the gas mask similar to what was used. Were you aware?

And Dr. Marcus testified, who sat also there, that one of the major flaws in your strategy was the fact that children and infants could not use gas [masks]. And also in the report of the events that took place, the Department of Justice report which you ordered, said, "Its impact on infants and children cannot be ignored because gas masks are not available for infants and younger children." Do you believe that that's something—a flaw that was made, a missed decision?

Reno: Yes. Let me begin first with your reference because it is so very important, as we consider something. Congressman, this has been, as I mentioned earlier—and you may not have been here—the single hardest decision of my life.

Rep. Mica: Well, I've heard that before. But were you aware that gas masks couldn't be used by the children and infants?

Reno: Mr. Chairman—

Rep. Mica: Were you aware—

Reno: If you would like to ask any other questions, I'll be happy to wait, but I need a little bit of time to answer, if I may.

Rep. Mica: Well, I have one other question I'd like to conclude with and you could supply me the answer in writing. In reading—I don't know if you read the autopsy reports, but my final question: In reading the autopsy reports of the women and children, I will always be haunted by what they contain. This past weekend I read a physician's report recounting how he found a closed and clenched woman's hand, and when he pried it open, he found the remains of an infant's hand. The doctor believed that many of the infants and children had their faces covered with wet towels because, in fact, they didn't have gas masks. But after hours of gassing undoubtedly tortured these infants before they were finally suffocated, according to the autopsy reports. Knowing this today, would you still proceed in the same manner? . . .

Reno: Mr. Mica, I really appreciate this opportunity to respond, because as I was telling you earlier—and I want you to understand because you, I don't think, can comprehend, if you talk to me about children, the fact that this instance will be etched on my mind for the rest of my life. Those children, no matter how they were found, the fact that they are dead is a tragedy that will be with me for the rest of my life. You do not have to talk in those terms. What we have got to do is to work together to avoid such tragedies for the future. . . .

This is the gas mask that the congressman is showing, but it's not very helpful, in terms of trying to understand what happened there, to just show gas masks. We've got to show the people what went into the process. And what went into the process was a dangerous situation which was getting more dangerous. What went into the process was extensive inquiry of toxicologists who consulted with others to try to find out whether this would be permanently harmful to the children.

We considered absolutely everything that we could. . . .

With respect to what we did to try to protect the children, our hope was that the children would come out, and that obviously, with the wind, with all the circumstances, the gas was not effective because there were people who went back into the compound. One of the agents who testified before you talked about the fact that there was no gas there when he went in to save her. All of these factors we tried to consider.

6

The FBI Should Not Have Used CS Gas

Alan A. Stone

In the following excerpts from a November 1993 report to the deputy attorney general, Dr. Alan A. Stone argues that the FBI should not have used CS gas, or 0-chlorobenzalmalononitrile, against the Branch Davidians. In particular, Stone says that although the FBI and Attorney General Janet Reno both insist the gas was used out of concern for the safety of the young children inside, a review of research on CS gas finds it to be highly dangerous, particularly to young children. In one study Stone cites, a young child suffered serious injury after three hours of exposure to the gas, and he points out that the FBI plan had called for the insertion of gas continuously for forty-eight hours. Stone concludes that using CS gas threatened, rather than protected, the safety of the children. Stone, who was one of several panelists appointed by the Justice and Treasury Departments to investigate and report on federal law enforcement in Waco, is a professor of psychiatry and law at Harvard University.

T he Justice Department's official investigation published on October 8th together with other information made available to the panelists [asked by the federal government to report on federal law enforcement in Waco] present convincing evidence that David Koresh ordered his followers to set the fire in which they perished. However, neither the official investigation nor the Dennis evaluation [a report commissioned by the Department of Justice] has provided a clear

Alan A. Stone, "Report and Recommendations Concerning the Handling of Incidents Such as the Branch Davidian Standoff in Waco, Texas," submitted to Deputy Attorney General Philip Heymann, November 10, 1993.

and probing account of the FBI tactics during the standoff and their possible relationship to the tragic outcome at Waco. This report therefore contains an account based on my own further review and interpretation of the facts.

I have concluded that the FBI command failed to give adequate consideration to their own behavioral science and negotiation experts. They also failed to make use of the Agency's own prior successful experience in similar circumstances. They embarked on a misguided and punishing law enforcement strategy that contributed to the tragic ending at Waco.

As a physician, I have concluded that there are serious unanswered questions about the basis for the decision to deploy toxic C.S. gas in a closed space where there were twenty-five children, many of them toddlers and infants. . . .

My concern as a member of the Behavioral Science Panel is whether the FBI strategy pursued at Waco in some way contributed to the tragedy which resulted in the death of twenty-five innocent children along with the adults. The Justice Department Investigation and the Dennis Evaluation [See "The FBI Deserves Praise, Not Blame," in this volume.] seem to agree with the FBI commander on the ground, who is convinced that nothing the FBI did or could have done would have changed the outcome. That is not my impression. . . .

Mounting Pressure

The pressure strategy as we now know it consisted of shutting off the compound's electricity, putting search lights on the compound all night, playing constant loud noise (including Tibetan prayer chants, the screaming sounds of rabbits being slaughtered, etc.), tightening the perimeter into a smaller and smaller circle in an overwhelming show of advancing armored force, and using C.S. gas. The constant stress overload is intended to lead to sleep-deprivation and psychological disorientation. In predisposed individuals the combination of physiological disruption and psychological stress can also lead to mood disturbances, transient hallucinations and paranoid ideation. If the constant noise exceeds 105 decibels, it can produce nerve deafness in children as well as in adults. Presumably, the tactical intent was to cause disruption and emotional chaos within the compound. The FBI hoped to break Koresh's hold over his followers. However, it may have solidified this unconventional group's unity in their common misery, a phenomenon familiar to victimology and group psychology.

It is difficult to believe that the U.S. government would deliberately plan to expose twenty-five children, most of them infants and toddlers, to C.S. gas for forty-eight hours.

When asked, the Justice Department was unaware whether the FBI had even questioned whether these intentional stresses would be particularly harmful to the many infants and children in the compound. Apparently, no one asked whether such deleterious measures were appropriate, either as a matter of law enforcement ethics or as a matter of morality, when innocent children were involved. This is not to suggest that the FBI decision-makers were cold-blooded tacticians who took no account of the children; in fact, there are repeated examples showing the concern of the agents, including the commander on the ground. Nevertheless, my opinion is that regardless of their apparent concern the FBI agents did not adequately consider the effects of these tactical actions on the children.

The Plan to Insert C.S. Gas

During U.S. military training, trainees are required to wear a gas mask when entering a tent containing C.S. gas. They then remove the mask and, after a few seconds in that atmosphere, are allowed to leave. I can testify from personal experience to the power of C.S. gas to quickly inflame eyes, nose, and throat, to produce choking, chest pain, gagging, and nausea in healthy adult males. It is difficult to believe that the U.S. government would deliberately plan to expose twenty-five children, most of them infants and toddlers, to C.S. gas for forty-eight hours. Although it is not discussed in the published reports, I have been told that the FBI believed that the Branch Davidians had gas masks and that this was one of the reasons for the plan of prolonged exposure. I have also been told that there was some protection available to the children, i.e covering places where the seal is incomplete with cold wet towels can adapt gas masks for children and perhaps for toddlers though not for infants. The official reports are silent about these issues and do not reveal what the FBI told the AG [Attorney General Janet Reno] about this matter, and whether she knew there might be unprotected children and infants in the compound.

The written information about the effects of C.S. gas which was presented to the AG has been shared with the panelists. We do not know whether she had time to read it. Based on my own medical knowledge and review of the scientific literature, the information supplied to the AG seems to minimize the potential harmful consequences for infants and children.

Scientific literature on C.S. gas is, however, surprisingly limited. In the sixties, the British Home Office, commissioned the Himsworth Report after complaints about the use of C.S. gas by British troops in Londonderry, Ireland. The report is said by its critics to understate the medical consequences. The published animal research on which the report is based acknowledged that at very high exposure, which the authors deemed unlikely, lethal effects were produced. The researchers assumed (as did the Himsworth Report) that C.S. gas would be used primarily in open spaces, to disperse crowds, and not in closed areas.

Minimizing the Risk

The AG's information emphasized the British experience and understated the potential health consequences in closed spaces. The AG also had a consultation with a physician; but the exact content of that discussion has not been reported, and the available summary is uninformative. The FBI commander on the ground assures me that the agency has detailed, ongoing expertise on C.S. gas and its medical consequences. If so, no such FBI information was supplied in the written material to the AG or subsequently to this panelist.

Based on my review, the American scientific literature on the toxic effects of C.S. gas on adults and children is also limited. Of course, there has been no deliberate experimentation on infants. The *Journal of the American Medical Association* published two articles in recent years in which physicians expressed concern about the use of C.S. gas on civilians, including children in South Korea and Israel. Anecdotal reports of the serious consequences of tear gas, however, [were] approved as early as 1956. Case reports indicate that prolonged exposure to tear gas in closed quarters causes chemical pneumonia and lethal pulmonary edema. According to a 1978 report, a disturbed adult died after only a half-hour exposure to C.S. gas in closed quarters. The clinical pathology found at autopsy in these cases is exactly what common medical understanding and ordinary pulmonary physiology predicts would follow prolonged exposure in closed quarters.

Ironically, while the most compelling factor used to justify the Waco plan was the safety of the children, the insertion of the C.S. gas, in my opinion, actually threatened the safety of the children.

The potential effects of C.S. gas are easily explained. C.S. gas causes among other things, irritation and inflammation of mucus membranes. The lung is a sack full of membranes. The inhalation of C.S. gas would eventually cause inflammation, and fluid would move across the membranes and collect in the alveoli, the tiny air sacks in the lungs that are necessary for breathing. The result is like pneumonia and can be lethal. Animal studies are available to confirm that C.S. gas has this effect on lung tissue. The Special Communication published by Physicians for Human Rights reported that its teams, investigating the use of C.S. gas in South Korea and Panama, found "skin burns, eye injuries and exacerbations of underlying heart and lung disease . . . on civilians at sites far removed from crowd gatherings." Dermatologists have reported blistering rashes on skin exposed to self-defense sprays, which use the same C.S. gas.

The medical literature does contain a clinical case history of a situation that closely approximates the expected Waco conditions. A normal four-month-old infant male was in a house into which police officers, in order to subdue a disturbed adult, fired canisters of C.S. gas. The unprotected child's exposure lasted two to three hours. Thereafter, he was immediately taken to an emergency room. His symptoms during the first twenty-four hours were upper respiratory; but, within forty-eight hours his face showed evidence of first degree burns, and he was in severe respiratory distress typical of chemical pneumonia. The infant had cyanosis, required urgent positive pressure pulmonary care, and was hospitalized for twenty-eight days. Other signs of toxicity appeared, including an enlarged liver. The infant's delayed onset of serious, life-threatening symptoms parallels the experience of animal studies done for the Himsworth Report. The infant's reactions reported in this case history were of a vastly different dimension than the information given the AG suggested.

Threatening the Safety of the Children

Of course, most people without gas masks would be driven by their instinct for survival from a C.S. gas–filled structure. But infants cannot run or even walk out of such an environment; and young children (many were toddlers) may be frightened or disoriented by this traumatic experience. The C.S. gas tactics, planned by the FBI and approved by the AG, would seem to give parents no choice. If they wanted to spare their inadequately protected children the intense and immediate suffering expectably caused by the C.S. gas, they would have had to take them out of the compound. Ironically, while the most compelling factor used to justify the Waco plan was the safety of the children, the insertion of the C.S. gas, in my opinion, actually threatened the safety of the children.

The Justice Department has informed me that because of the high winds at Waco, the C.S. gas was dispersed; they believe it played no part in the death by suffocation, revealed at autopsy, of most of the infants, toddlers, and children. The commander on the ground, however, is of the opinion that the C.S. gas did have some effect, because the wind did not begin to blow strongly until two hours after he ordered the operation to begin. As yet, there has been no report as to whether the children whose bodies were found in the bunker were equipped with gas masks. Whatever the actual effects may have been, I find it hard to accept a deliberate plan to insert C.S. gas for forty-eight hours in a building with so many children. It certainly makes it more difficult to believe that the health and safety of the children was our primary concern.

Chapter 2

Lingering Questions

1

The FBI May Have Accidentally Started the Fire

Richard L. Sherrow

In the following excerpt from an affidavit, Richard L. Sherrow says that the fire that destroyed Mount Carmel and killed most of those inside could have been started accidentally by the FBI. Sherrow begins by noting that Mount Carmel was highly flammable, both because of its haphazard construction and because it contained a lot of stored fuel. He then recounts the day of the fire and discusses the FBI's introduction of CS gas. According to Sherrow, the totality of available evidence is compatible with a theory in which the fire started with an overturned lantern, perhaps upset by a Combat Engineer Vehicle (CEV) hitting the building, and then spread quickly due to the presence of flammable material and high wind. Sherrow also argues that the FBI, by using the CEVs to dismantle parts of the building, and by pumping in very high levels of CS gas, may have made it harder for those inside to escape once the fire broke out. Sherrow is a former fire and explosion investigator with the Bureau of Alcohol, Tobacco, and Firearms and a retired senior explosive ordnance disposal technician for the U.S. Army.

I have made a preliminary investigation into the cause, origin, nature and growth of the fire which consumed the Mount Carmel Center near Waco, Texas, on April 19, 1993,

Richard L. Sherrow, "Fire Investigator's Civil Suit Affidavit on Origin of April 19, 1993, Fire at Mount Carmel," www.carolmoore.net, January 17, 1996.

and where members of the Branch Davidian religion perished as a result of said fire. This preliminary investigation was based upon the Forward-Looking Infrared (FLIR) video [which detects heat], still photographs extracted from the FLIR, still photographs taken from the air and from the ground during the fire, broadcast news video, videography taken by a private investigator while the government was in control of the Mount Carmel Center, signed statements and interviews of Branch Davidians who survived the fire, official reports and case notes of federal and state law enforcement agents, the reports of the United States' fire investigators (namely Paul Gray and James Quiontere) and from my own personal inspection of the fire site.

Based upon this preliminary investigation, I am able to conclude, within my professional opinion, that it is consistent with this evidence that the fire originated from a single point and spread throughout the Mount Carmel structure. It is also consistent with evidence that the original fire was started by a M728 Combat Engineer Vehicle (CEV) striking the southeast corner tower of Mount Carmel. . . .

A Highly Flammable Building

Mount Carmel Center was a multi-storied, wood-frame building of irregular construction. It was built of about half used lumber and building materials cannibalized from houses that had existed on the property previously and from new materials purchased for its construction. The building was constructed haphazardly over time without any attention to fire safety. Some of the building's interior lacked wallboard or finishing. Those areas of the building which had been finished were completed with highly flammable materials.

Contained within the building on the first floor were the living quarters, dining and kitchen areas, several storage rooms, a chapel and gymnasium. A four-story tower was located near the center of the structure and contained a reinforced-concrete room used to house a walk-in cooler for food storage. This concrete structure was built in the 1930's and had survived a previous fire some years before.

The second floor was contiguous over the first and also contained living quarters. Both corners of the building in front contained a third story. Moreover, the four-story tower had a fourth floor directly over the third.

Foundation, slabs and piers were homemade with unreinforced concrete and did not contribute significantly to the building's resistance to mechanical shock. The roof was of decked plywood construction, overlaid with asphalt composition roofing materials.

External electrical power was turned off to the structure prior to the fire but a diesel generator of unknown capacity was present within the structure and had been known to be energized intermittently between February 28 and April 19, 1993. Moreover, several storage areas and rooms were known to contain large amounts of highly flammable and combustible materials, including, but not limited to, gasoline, kerosene, lamp oil, Coleman lantern fuel, paint, petroleum distillates, tar and roofing materials, acetylene and oxygen containers, gunpowder, metal shavings, and a large quantity of small arms ammunition.

Internal heating and cooking fires were provided by improvised wood-burning stoves and propane fueled gas ranges, respectively. Due to the lack of external electrical power, internal lighting was accomplished with Coleman-type gas pressurized lanterns and glass oil-burning wick lamps.

It is known that a large, commercial-type gas range was located in the kitchen/dining area adjacent to the four-story tower. This range was fed by a large, 100 pound propane tank located externally to the dining room. The propane was conducted through the wall at that location by a conduit pipe. The tank appeared to be nearly full of propane as evidenced by a spectacular boiling liquid expanding vapor explosion (BLEVE) during the fire.

Mount Carmel Center was occupied as a multi-family residential building with shared common areas, including a commercial-sized kitchen, and compartmented into many smaller rooms used for personal quarters. . . .

The Day of the Fire

On April 19, 1993, at approximately 6:00 A.M., agents of the Federal Bureau of Investigation began executing a plan to introduce a riot control agent, ortho-chlorobenzal-malononitrile (CS). . . .

During the next six hours, the FBI utilized M728 CEVs to breach the outer walls of the building and to inject CS. A CEV is a large armored vehicle, weighing in excess of 50 tons, is equipped with a 165mm demolition gun and is modification of the M60A1 Main Battle Tank. The CS was injected by use of a Mark V delivery device. The MK-V delivery device consisted of several bottles of pressurized carbon dioxide which was used to entrain the particulate CS in a gaseous stream. This stream was injected into the structure through a nozzle located on the end of a boom connected to the CEV.

In addition to the CS injection utilizing the Mark-V delivery systems on the CEVs, FBI agents in Bradley Infantry Fighting Vehicles (BIFV) fired SGA-400 Ferret barricade penetrating cartridges into windows and areas not reachable by the CEVs. A Ferret is a 40 mm projectile containing particulate CS and a liquid suspension agent, methylene chloride. The Ferret is a non-pyrotechnic munition specifically designed for barricade situations. At least 400, and possibly more, of these Ferret rounds were fired in and at Branch Davidians during the breaching and CS insertion operation.

> *I am able to conclude, within my professional opinion, that it is consistent with this evidence that the fire originated from a single point and spread throughout the Mount Carmel structure.*

Besides the SGA-400 Ferret cartridges, information from documents obtained from the FBI through the United States Department of Justice indicates that military pyrotechnic munitions may have been fired into Mount Carmel. Documents disclosed indicate that agents could not penetrate either the underground shelter roof or the top of the rear four-story tower with Ferrets. Therefore, they fired at least one "military" round and referred to this munition as a "bubblehead." As a retired U.S. Army senior explosive ordnance disposal technician, I am unaware of the nomenclature and function of a "bubblehead" nor can I find any reference to such a munition in official military publications. However, I am familiar with a device known as a "bunker buster," which is a munition about the size of a softball and designed to penetrate fortifications. I recall that this munition was of foreign manufacture and filled with plasticized high explosive (HEP). It may have had other fillers, including chemical riot control agents. The exact identity of a "bubblehead" would have to be determined before any possible contribution to the fire could be established.

In the event that members of the Branch Davidians contemplated or began to execute a mass suicide, it was the plan of the FBI Hostage Rescue Team (HRT) "to disrupt any suicide attempt with flash-bangs." "Flash-bang" generically refers to pyrotechnic stun munitions designed to temporarily incapacitate or disorient personnel by producing a loud report and blinding flash. These munitions contain an explosive/incendiary pyrotechnic composition. A number of these munitions manufactured by the Nico Corporation were known to be fired during the 51-day standoff and were in the possession of the FBI HRT on April 19, 1993. Use of stun munitions in barricade situations is extremely hazardous due to the potential of causing an accidental fire. . . .

It is known that many of the Branch Davidians were in possession of protective masks. Therefore, the effective use of CS would require the introduction of quantities of these agents far in excess of that required to deter trained troops (10 mg/m^3 for CS) and well past the levels required to pose an immediate danger to life and health (2 mg/m^3 for CS). Calculations by engineers for an independent casualty laboratory, Failure Analysis, Inc., have concluded that the average concentration of CS inside of Mount Carmel was 10 to 90 times that necessary to deter trained troops (100 to 900 mg/m^3). In my professional opinion and based upon my experience with the use of these riot control agents, the concentration of CS introduced was designed to overcome the protective masks by rapidly debilitating their filters and posed an immediate threat to the life, health and safety of those inside Mount Carmel, especially the unprotected children. . . .

A Possible Cause of the Fire

After reviewing the evidence, I have reached a preliminary conclusion on the cause, origin, nature and growth of the fire. This opinion is only preliminary as much additional evidence is required before any conclusion can be reached which has a confidence level greater than possible.

1. The fire originated in the southeast corner tower from the tipping of a lit Coleman-type lantern which fell onto combustible materials, most likely bedding materials, as the room was utilized as sleeping quarters, and was most

likely caused by violent contact or mechanical shock associated with the CEV removing the corner of the southeast tower directly under the point of origin. The time of origin could have been as late as 12:06:24 P.M., but could have been earlier.

2. The fire smoldered, producing toxic and combustible gases in the room. As these gases collected, the combustible materials ignited, producing visible heat and flame. This ignition is first detected by the FLIR at 12:07:41 but may have been burning for some time prior to this.

3. A flashover of the second floor room of the southeast corner tower occurs. This appears on the FLIR at 12:08:56 but appears to be already in progress. The flashover could not have been observed earlier because the FLIR operator had the southeast corner tower out of the field of view.

4. At the time of ignition, there were ambient winds in excess of 25 knots gusting to 40 knots (28.7 to 46 mph). These extremely high winds are quite significant with respect to the fire growth and spread. The angle of the wind to the structure, from southeast to northwest, is in direct line with the fire growth and propagation as would be expected.

5. There were two large holes made in the front of the structure by the CEVs; one through the front of the double doors and one directly in the center of the building. Both of these breaching operations caused considerable structural damage to the flooring of the second story, opening that story to the one below. Moreover, high winds were able to enter through these breaches and create a venturi, or wind-tunnel effect, in the transverse corridors in the front of the building. This venturi effect created a negative pressure zone in the interior and pulled air from the southeast corner of the building toward the west and north sides. The velocity of the airstream was considerable according to eyewitness survivors. Further, an additional venturi is created by the demolition of the gymnasium and breaching of the exterior wall directly behind the chapel on the southeast side of the structure.

6. Approximately ten minutes earlier, CEV-1 attempted to make a through and through penetration from the front of the structure to the rear. During this penetration, CEV-1 struck the reinforced concrete structure at the base of the center four-story tower wherein most of the women and children had taken refuge. This deep penetration severely

disrupted the building structure and opened the ceiling of the dining area to the second story hallway.

7. As the fire flashes over in the southeast corner tower, the fire is pulled into the second story transverse hallway by the venturi created by the ambient winds. Hot, burning and combustible material is sucked by the wind and negative pressure into the hallway and transported rapidly throughout. Once these firebrands encounter the obstructions in the middle of the building from the CEV-1 penetration, they are ducted into the dining area by the breach in the floor.

8. At 12:08:49, approximately a little over one minute, a heat signature is observed at the rear of the dining area which appears to be fire. Most of the heat signature appears to be outside of the building at this point. The signature is unique in that comparisons with visible light video show it producing a white vapor which is consistent with burning propane. Moreover, much combustible material, petroleum distillates, paints, and lantern fuel were stored in the rear of the dining area according to witnesses.

9. In addition to the venturi ducting down the transverse front corridor, the fire grows because of the flashover from the southeast corner tower fire and spreads rapidly through the attic of the adjoining chapel. A surviving witness has stated that he heard a cry of fire coming from the second floor and went up into the chapel attic to investigate, crossing a causeway built over the rafters. The chapel attic and causeway were contiguous with the second floor front corridor and separated only by a blanket. When the witness arrived at the junction of the transverse corridor hallway and the chapel attic, he observed a "wall of fire" traveling down the corridor. . . .

10. The fire growth in the chapel was accelerated by the presence of petroleum distillates and lantern fuels. Surviving witnesses stated that approximately one dozen cans of Coleman lantern fuel were moved from the front door area to the chapel to prevent their destruction by CEV penetration.

11. Once the chapel was fully involved, the fire then spread to the gymnasium area. The northwest side of the gymnasium had been completely destroyed by action of CEV-2. This reduced the surface to mass ratio of the fuel (building materials) such that the fire was able to secure a rapid purchase and accelerate its growth. In addition, the action of CEV-2 in this area may have crushed numerous

fuel and propane containers, aiding in the rapid propagation and growth of the fire. Such fuel appears to show on the FLIR as dark spots and it is known from surviving Davidians that fuel and propane containers were there.

12. Abetted by high winds, the fire rapidly spreads, completely destroying the rest of the structure.

Trapped Inside

The conclusions of the government's experts assert that the occupants of the building could have escaped the fire had they wanted to. . . .

As noted above, the breaching operations of the CEVs caused considerable disruption and mechanical failure to large portions of the structure; in fact, the entire southeast side of the building was knocked off its foundation by action of the CEVs. This disruption probably created multiple hazards including entrapment, crushing, and restrictions of egress and community between floors. Early breaching operations are known to have occluded access to the trap door leading to an underground shelter. Eyewitness testimony and statements establish that CEV operations destroyed or significantly damaged the two stairways leading from the upper floors, trapping those occupants to the upper levels of the structure. Moreover, doors were known to be sprung and were unable to be opened because of structural distortion.

The noise generated by the high winds blowing through the building and that from the unmuffled CEV engines also would inhibit the spread of an alarm. In fact, eyewitness interviews establish that the alarm of fire, first broadcast from the site of origin, was not transmitted to the other occupants because of noise interference and attenuation or acoustic disruption due to structural damage.

Many of the fire victims, mostly the women and children, died inside or in close proximity to the concrete structure at the base of the four-story tower. This is the same structure which had been in the path of CEV-1 during its deep penetration. The actions of CEV-1 in making this penetration had bulldozed large amounts of material, if not against, then in front of the door, limiting egress. Witnesses believe that many of the women took their children into the walk-in cooler to protect them from the effects of the CS. The cooler had an air-tight door and was not electrically energized.

The injection of CS had occurred numerous times during the day. Each injection filled at least part of the building with a dense cloud of particulate matter, limiting breathing and visibility. When flashover occurred in the southeast corner tower, the combustion products were rapidly distributed throughout the building. This initial warning was ignored by some occupants because they mistook the fire products as another CS injection, delaying their apprehension of danger and severely limiting their time for escape.

As with all fires, the combustible products, including carbon monoxide, carbon dioxide, hydrogen cyanide (all of which were found in the Branch Davidian victims who died by smoke inhalation), deprive the brain of oxygen and cause confusion, limiting a fire victim's ability to apprehend danger and to execute a plan of escape. Moreover, the toxic combustion products produced by the injection of methylene chloride into the structure, phosgene (PG) and chlorine (Cl) gas, could have rendered large numbers of people unconscious and prevented their escape from the fire. According to the Material Safety Data sheet and hazardous chemical data published for methylene chloride, the vapors can readily accumulate and can cause unconsciousness and death in confined and poorly ventilated spaces; it is an eye, skin and respiratory tract irritant. Toxic, methylene chloride is a narcotic in high concentrations and is metabolized by the body to form carbon monoxide. Moreover, methylene chloride is flammable in its vapor state, and may have contributed to the spread and rapid growth of the fire. . . .

Some consideration must also be given to the psychodynamics of the group considering their subjugation to psychological pressure tactics, sleep deprivation and general apprehension and fear of the government agents outside contributing to their delay to exit the building. . . .

Thus, the psychological condition of the occupants after 51 days of siege, the excessive introduction of CS and any attendant toxic effects, general and pervasive fear of external conditions and induced group social dynamics most likely led to a delayed perception of danger with tragic consequences.

2

The Allegations Against the Federal Government Are False

John C. Danforth

In the summer of 1999, credible evidence surfaced that the FBI had used pyrotechnic rounds on April 19, 1993, something the bureau had long denied, and there was the suggestion that these may have been responsible for the fire. Also, there were continued allegations that FBI agents had fired upon Mount Carmel on April 19, which the bureau also denied, and that U.S. military forces had been involved at Waco. (The Posse Comitatus Act bars the military from taking part in civilian law enforcement.) In response to these and other allegations, Attorney General Janet Reno appointed John C. Danforth to lead an investigation. In July 2000, Danforth released an interim report that was widely reported as having exonerated the government. In this document, excerpted below, Danforth concludes that the Branch Davidians, not the FBI, started the fire, that no FBI agents fired at Mount Carmel on April 19, and that U.S. Armed Forces did not participate illegally at Waco. Danforth also concludes that although the FBI had made false statements regarding whether any pyrotechnic devices had been used, neither Attorney General Reno nor FBI director William S. Sessions was involved in a cover-up. In a follow-up report released later, Danforth concluded that "a few government employees did knowingly conceal the FBI's use of pyrotechnic tear gas rounds" but that their actions did not constitute a cover-up by the bureau, the Department of

John C. Danforth, "Interim Report to the Deputy Attorney General Concerning the 1993 Confrontation at the Mt. Carmel Complex, Waco, Texas," July 21, 2000. Pursuant to Order No. 2256-99 of the Attorney General.

Justice, or by the federal government generally. Danforth is a former U.S. senator from Missouri.

The Office of Special Counsel has undertaken an exhaustive investigation into allegations of grave misconduct by employees of the United States government. In essence, the charges are that on April 19, 1993, federal agents caused the fire which destroyed the Branch Davidian complex and killed many Davidians who remained in it, directed gunfire at the complex, illegally employed the armed forces of the United States to assault the complex, and then covered up the alleged misconduct.

To date, the investigation has lasted ten months, employed 74 personnel, and cost approximately $12 million. The Office of Special Counsel has interviewed 849 witnesses, reviewed over two million pages of documents, and examined thousands of pounds of physical evidence. As a result of this effort, the Office of Special Counsel states the following conclusions with certainty:

The government of the United States and its agents are not responsible for the April 19, 1993, tragedy at Waco. The government:

(a) did not cause the fire;

(b) did not direct gunfire at the Branch Davidian complex; and

(c) did not improperly employ the armed forces of the United States.

Responsibility for the tragedy of Waco rests with certain members of the Branch Davidians and their leader, David Koresh, who:

(a) shot and killed four ATF agents on February 28, 1993, and wounded 20 others;

(b) refused to exit the complex peacefully during the 51-day standoff that followed the ATF raid despite extensive efforts and concessions by negotiators for the Federal Bureau of Investigation ("FBI");

(c) directed gunfire at FBI agents who were inserting tear gas into the complex on April 19, 1993;

(d) spread fuel throughout the main structure of the complex and ignited it in at least three places causing the fire which resulted in the deaths of those Branch Davidians not killed by their own gunfire; and

(e) killed some of their own people by gunfire, including at least five children.

While the Special Counsel has concluded that the United States government is not responsible for the tragedy at Waco on April 19, 1993, the Special Counsel states with equal certainty that an FBI agent fired three pyrotechnic tear gas rounds at 8:08 A.M. on April 19, 1993, at the concrete construction pit approximately 75 feet from the living quarters of the Davidian complex. The pyrotechnic tear gas rounds did not start the fire that consumed the complex four hours later. The failure of certain government officials to acknowledge the use of the pyrotechnic tear gas rounds until August of 1999 constitutes, at best, negligence in the handling of evidence and information and, at worst, a criminal effort to cover up the truth. As more fully described below, the Special Counsel has made substantial progress in resolving the coverup issue, but the investigation is not yet complete. . . .

4. Was there any illegal or improper use of the armed forces of the United States in connection with events leading up to the deaths of the Branch Davidians on April 19, 1993?

The Office of Special Counsel investigated allegations that members of the armed forces of the United States violated the law by participating directly in the Waco law enforcement operation. Allegations made against the armed forces included claims that its members shot at the Davidians from helicopters on February 28, 1993, infiltrated the complex during the standoff, placed explosive devices in the complex, offered to kidnap Koresh, and shot at the Davidians from positions around government vehicles on April 19, 1993. These allegations proved entirely meritless.

The armed forces of the United States did not violate any civil or criminal statute in connection with their activities at Waco in 1993. While the armed forces of the United States provided extensive support for law enforcement agencies, including reconnaissance, equipment, training, advice, and medical assistance, they were careful in their conduct and well-advised legally as they determined exactly what support to provide. In fact, in at least two instances, law enforcement agencies solicited assistance from the armed forces that the armed forces either rejected or scaled back due to concern about remaining within the bounds of federal law. . . .

1. Did agents of the United States start or contribute to the spread of the fire that caused the death of Branch Davidians on April 19, 1993?

Government agents did not start or materially contribute to the spread of the fire. During the morning of April 19, 1993, several Davidians spread accelerants throughout the main structure of the complex, and started fires in at least three locations. The evidence indicates that many of the Davidians did not want to escape the fire. Indeed, while government agents risked their lives to save Davidians from the fire, one Davidian tried to re-enter the burning complex to die. When an FBI agent questioned this Davidian regarding the location of the children, the Davidian refused to answer. A Davidian who exited the complex during the fire stated that he witnessed others make no effort to leave the complex. Another Davidian expressed remorse that she had not perished in the fire with the rest of the group.

The following evidence demonstrates that the Davidians started the fire:

(a) Title III Intercepts [court-authorized wiretaps]. Davidian conversations intercepted through the use of concealed listening devices inside the complex from April 17 to April 19 indicate that the Davidians started the fire. An April 17 intercept records Davidians discussing how they could prevent fire trucks from reaching the complex. An April 18 intercept records a conversation between Steven Schneider and other Davidians indicating a conspiracy to start a fire. During that conversation, Schneider joked that another Davidian had always wanted to be a "charcoal briquette." Another Davidian stated that, "I know there's nothing like a good fire. . . ." On April 19, between the beginning of the gas insertion operation at approximately 6:00 A.M. and approximately 7:25 A.M., the Title III intercepts recorded the following statements: "Need fuel;" "Do you want it poured?;" "Have you poured it yet?;" "Did you pour it yet?;" "David said pour it right?;" "David said we have to get the fuel on;" "We want the fuel;" "They got some fuel around here;" "Have you got the fuel . . . the fuel ready?;" "I've already poured it;" "It's already poured;" "Yeah . . . we've been pouring it;" "Pouring it already;" "Real quickly you can order the fire yes;" "You got to put the fuel in there too;" "We've got it poured already;" "Is there a way to spread fuel in there?;" "So we only light it first when they

come in with the tank right . . . right as they're coming in;" "That's secure . . . we should get more hay in here;" "You have to spread it all so get started ok?" These statements precede the sighting of fire by several hours, which is further proof that the Davidians intended to set fire to the complex well in advance of actually lighting the fires.

Much closer to the time of the fire, from approximately 11:17 A.M. to 12:04 P.M., Title III intercepts recorded the following statements from inside the complex: "Do you think I could light this soon?;" "I want a fire on the front . . . you two can go;" "Keep that fire going . . . keep it." The only plausible explanation for these comments is that some of the Davidians were executing their plan to start a fire.

The experts concluded without question that people inside the complex started the fire in at least three places.

(*b*) *Admissions of Branch Davidians.* Davidians who survived the fire have acknowledged that other Davidians started the fire. Graeme Craddock, a Davidian who survived the fire, told the Office of Special Counsel in 1999 that he observed other Davidians pouring fuel in the chapel area of the complex on April 19, 1993. He further stated that he saw another Davidian, Mark Wendel, arrive from the second floor yelling: "Light the fire." Davidian Clive Doyle told the Texas Rangers on April 20, 1993, that Davidians had spread Coleman fuel in designated locations throughout the complex, although he declined to state who specifically lit the fires.

(*c*) *Statements of Government Witnesses.* Observations by government witnesses support the conclusion that the Davidians started the fire. FBI agents who had the opportunity to observe activity within the Branch Davidian complex on April 19, using field glasses or spotting scopes, saw Davidians engaged in activity which they later concluded to be pouring fuel to start a fire. Some of these sightings were noted contemporaneously by the agents in FBI logs. Also, an FBI agent observed an unidentified Davidian ignite a fire in the front door area of the complex shortly after noon. This observation was also reported contemporaneously.

(*d*) *Expert Fire Analysis.* Fire experts also agree that Davidians started the fire. The Office of Special Counsel interviewed the experts who performed the original, on-scene fire investigation and analysis. The Office of Special Counsel also retained two fire experts, one to review the work product of the previous investigators and to examine independently the photographic and physical evidence, and the other to analyze the spread of the fire throughout the complex. In addition, the Office of Special Counsel retained an expert to determine whether the tear gas, a combination of methylene chloride and ortho-chlorobenzylmalonitrile (commonly referred to as "CS gas"), reached concentration levels in the complex that were sufficiently high to have caused or contributed to the rapid spread of the fire.

Relying upon photographs, records of previous on-site investigative activity (such as the use of an accelerant detection dog), physical evidence, computer models and Forward Looking Infrared ("FLIR" [which detects heat]) tapes, the experts concluded without question that people inside the complex started the fire in at least three places—the second floor of the southeast corner of the main structure of the complex, the stage area at the rear of the chapel, and the kitchen/cafeteria area. The experts further concluded that the CS and methylene chloride did not start or contribute to the spread of the fire. . . .

2. Did agents of the United States direct gunfire at the Branch Davidian complex on April 19, 1993?

No employee of the United States fired a gunshot at the Branch Davidian complex on April 19, 1993. To the contrary, while the Davidians fired upon government agents throughout the morning of April 19, government agents did not return gunfire. Indeed, the FBI had the authority to return fire under the law and its deadly force policy, but did not do so.

In arriving at these conclusions, the Office of Special Counsel relied upon the following evidence:

(a) FLIR Testing and Analysis. Virtually the only evidence cited by those claiming government agents fired shots into the complex on April 19, 1993, are the FLIR videos recorded by the FBI Nightstalker aircraft from approximately 10:42 A.M. to 12:41 P.M. on that day. In fact, however, this evidence strongly supports the conclusion that no employee of the United States fired a shot on April 19.

The FLIR tapes show 57 flashes, emanating principally

from alleged Davidian positions inside or on top of the complex. . . .

Based on a detailed analysis of the shape, duration and location of 57 flashes noted on the 1993 FLIR tapes, and a comparison of those flashes with flashes recorded on the March 2000 FLIR test tape, the expert retained by the Office of Special Counsel concluded with certainty that each of the flashes noted on the 1993 tapes resulted from a reflection off debris on or around the complex. . . .

(d) Statements of Government Witnesses. The United States government has maintained consistently since April 19, 1993, that no government agent fired a single shot at the Davidian complex on April 19. . . .

Office of Special Counsel attorneys and investigators asked government representatives who were present at the complex on April 19 (or otherwise involved in the Waco confrontation) not only whether they fired weapons, but also whether they saw any other government person fire a weapon, and whether they even heard discussion or rumor that any government agent engaged in gunfire. Not a single one of the hundreds of government witnesses stated that he or she had any knowledge suggesting that any government agent fired at the Davidians on April 19.

The government did not fire at the Davidians
. . . the Davidians fired at the government and
shot themselves.

Numerous government witnesses did, however, see or hear gunfire emanating from the complex toward government positions at various times during the morning of April 19. In addition, shortly after the start of the fire, at least four witnesses heard rhythmic bursts of gunfire coming from within the complex, which is consistent with the conclusion that the Davidians were deliberately shooting each other. The eyewitness accounts of government personnel, therefore, indicate that the government did not fire at the Davidians, but that the Davidians fired at the government and shot themselves. . . .

(a) Did government officials intentionally conceal the FBI's use of pyrotechnic tear gas rounds from Congress, the courts, counsel for the Davidians, and others from April 1993 until August

1999? As detailed earlier, the FBI fired three pyrotechnic tear gas rounds at the concrete construction pit outside the main structure of the complex shortly after 8:00 A.M. on April 19, 1993. The firing of these rounds neither started nor contributed to the spread of the fire that consumed the complex four hours later. However, until August of 1999, FBI and Department of Justice officials repeatedly denied that the FBI had used *any* such device during the tear gassing operation. These statements were false, and the failure to acknowledge the use of pyrotechnic tear gas rounds for more than six years has greatly undermined public confidence in government. . . .

A. *Statements of the Attorney General.* The Office of Special Counsel has concluded that Attorney General Reno did not knowingly cover up the use of pyrotechnic tear gas rounds by the FBI. The evidence is overwhelming that, prior to the execution of the gassing plan, she sought and received assurances from the FBI that it would not use pyrotechnic tear gas rounds. The evidence is equally conclusive that the briefing materials and other information she received after the fact stated that the FBI had not used pyrotechnic tear gas rounds at Waco. Any misstatement that she made was inadvertent and occurred after diligent efforts on her part to learn the truth. The Office of Special Counsel has completed its investigation of Attorney General Reno, found her to be without direct fault for any false statements that she may have made, and will not pursue any action against her.

B. *FBI Statements in 1993.* The Office of Special Counsel has also concluded that FBI Director [William] Sessions did not knowingly mislead Congress in 1993 regarding the FBI's use of pyrotechnics at Waco. Director Sessions' statement that CS gas was chosen because it could be used without pyrotechnics was true. He simply did not know that three pyrotechnic military tear gas rounds had also been used on the morning of April 19. Similarly, when [FBI Spokesman Robert] Ricks gave his press briefing immediately after the fire, he did not know that any pyrotechnic tear gas rounds had been used. The FBI's plan clearly called only for the use of Ferret tear gas rounds which are non-pyrotechnic, and no one had told Ricks that the HRT [Hostage Rescue Team] had used pyrotechnic tear gas rounds that morning. . . .

D. *The FBI Hostage Rescue Team.* In November 1993, the criminal trial team prosecuting the Davidians interviewed members of the HRT at Quantico, Virginia. Those who knew of the use of the military tear gas rounds, including HRT commander [Richard] Rogers, admitted openly to the criminal trial team that the FBI had fired the military tear gas rounds at the concrete construction pit on April 19. In addition, HRT agent Robert Hickey acknowledged the use of the military tear gas rounds and their capacity to start a fire in a memorandum to an FBI lawyer in February 1996. HRT members candidly admitted to the Office of Special Counsel that they had used these rounds. There was clearly no attempt on their part to conceal the use of military tear gas rounds.

HRT commander Rogers did, however, sit silently behind Attorney General Reno when she testified to Congress in April 1993 that she had sought and received assurances that the gas and its means of delivery would be non-pyrotechnic. Rogers claims that he was not paying attention and did not even hear her when she made this statement, and Attorney General Reno notes that her statement was technically true because she sought and received the assurances *before* the operation. Similarly, Rogers attended the 1993 testimony of FBI Director Sessions, and did not correct misimpressions left by Sessions' statement that the FBI had chosen CS gas because it could be delivered without pyrotechnics. Rogers' failure to correct the misleading implications of the testimony of Attorney General Reno and Director Sessions was a significant omission that contributed to the public perception of a coverup and that permitted a false impression to persist for several years. Rogers attended the congressional hearings precisely to ensure that Congress was provided with accurate information. Instead, in the terms of the Attorney General's Order to the Special Counsel, Rogers "allow[ed] others to make . . . misleading statements." The Office of Special Counsel, however, will not pursue any further investigation of Rogers or any member of the HRT.

3

Waco's Unprosecuted Crimes and Unanswered Questions

Timothy Lynch

In the following piece, Timothy Lynch argues that there is very good reason to think that federal agents committed crimes during the Waco standoff for which they are not being prosecuted. Furthermore, he says, there are numerous unanswered questions about the initial raid, the standoff, the final conflagration and the conduct of federal employees that deserve to be investigated. As Lynch sees it, the events at Waco, which he calls the most controversial law enforcement operation in modern American history, point to the dangers of giving government too much power and trusting it blindly. Lynch is director of the Cato Institute's Project on Criminal Justice.

On April 19, 1993, agents of the Federal Bureau of Investigation used tanks to assault a building that contained 76 men, women, and children. The tanks rammed holes through the walls of the building and sprayed tear gas inside. Because the adults in the building had gas masks, the FBI's tactical objective was to gas the children so as to prompt the parents to gather them up and flee the structure. After several hours of gassing, a fire broke out and almost everyone in the building died. That incident, which is now commonly referred to as Waco because it took place a few miles outside of Waco, Texas, has become the most controversial law en-

Timothy Lynch, "No Confidence: An Unofficial Account of the Waco Incident," *Policy Analysis*, April 9, 2001, pp. 2, 9–14. Copyright © 2001 by the Cato Institute. Reproduced by permission.

forcement operation in modern American history.

For years questions have lingered about whether the federal government was completely forthright about what happened at Waco. Did the people in the building really commit mass suicide? Or was it closer to murder, with federal agents abusing their power and then covering up their misdeeds? The "official" investigation of the Waco incident was headed by former Missouri senator John C. Danforth, whose report essentially exonerated the federal government of wrongdoing. The factual record, however, does not support Danforth's sweeping exoneration. On the contrary, it raises deeply disturbing questions not only about the tactics used at Waco but, more generally, about the mindset often found in America's increasingly militarized law enforcement agencies. . . .

Crimes at Waco

In a free society, a person who commits a crime is not exempt from investigation or prosecution merely because he works for the government, wears a uniform, and carries a badge. If that basic legal principle is taken seriously, it is not extraordinarily difficult to identify crimes that were committed by government agents at Waco in 1993.

ATF Agents Attacked TV Cameraman Dan Mulloney. On February 28, 1993, several ATF agents physically attacked a local television cameraman named Dan Mulloney. Mulloney was on the scene at Mt. Carmel covering the ATF raid for KWTX-TV. After the firefight, Mulloney was filming the ATF agents as they were retreating from the Davidian property. When several ATF agents noticed what he was doing, they screamed obscenities at him and actually punched and kicked him while others tried to steal his camera. Because Mulloney kept his camera rolling during the entire episode, this assault, battery, and attempted theft are captured on film. The evidence is thus overwhelming. It is a crime for an ordinary citizen to punch and kick a cameraman. It is no less a crime for ATF agents to do so, yet they were never criminally prosecuted.

Although this incident lasted for approximately one minute, the film footage is telling because it clearly shows that certain ATF agents felt perfectly justified in breaking the law.

ATF Agents Lied to Federal Investigators. To avoid an actual or perceived conflict of interest, Texas Rangers were asked to conduct an investigation of possible criminal wrongdoing by ATF agents. The Rangers were deputized as U.S. marshals and were asked to look for possible federal criminal violations. In sworn testimony before Congress, one of the investigating Rangers said that the two ATF raid commanders, Phil Chojnacki and Chuck Sarabyn, lied to him about what had happened on February 28, 1993. Because ordinary citizens are sent to jail for lying to federal investigators, the Ranger recommended that Chojnacki and Sarabyn be indicted and prosecuted. The Ranger gave his recommendation to federal prosecutor Bill Johnston. Johnston, in turn, referred the matter to the Department of Justice in Washington, which took no action.

In October 1994 the Treasury Department did suspend Chojnacki and Sarabyn from active duty for making false statements, but they were subsequently reinstated with full back pay and had the entire Waco incident expunged from their personnel records.

FBI Agents Fired More than 350 Ferret Rounds into Mt. Carmel. The FBI has always admitted firing more than 350 ferret rounds at the Davidians on April 19, 1993. The ferrets were fired into the residence from hand-held grenade launchers. Ferret rounds are fired at such a speed that they are capable of causing serious injury or death. Government documents and testimony euphemistically refer to the "delivery" of tear gas into the residence—as if the ferrets were delivered by United Parcel Service. Firing ferret rounds into a building without knowing which adults are threatening and which are not—and without knowing where children are located—manifests an extreme indifference to human life. Such indifference is not only unconscionable but criminal.

Special Prosecutor Danforth's investigation of the Waco incident tried to draw a distinction between "bad judgment" and "bad acts." When he was appointed special prosecutor, Danforth promised that he would not file charges against any government employee for exercising bad judgment. But the firing of ferret rounds on April 19th cannot be brushed aside as simply poor judgment. A police officer exercises bad judgment if he uses the siren on his car to speed through traffic to a dental appointment. What happened at Waco was far more serious.

An ordinary citizen would not be accused of mere "bad

judgment" if he used a grenade launcher to fire ferret rounds into a nursery school. If a child were struck and killed by one of the ferrets, the citizen could face murder charges. Even if the citizen intended only to scare people, he could be held liable for second degree murder because his actions consciously disregarded a substantial and unjustifiable risk of harm to others.

In a free society, a person who commits a crime is not exempt from investigation or prosecution merely because he works for the government, wears a uniform, and carries a badge.

FBI agents might have been justified in firing ferret rounds into all of the windows of the Mt. Carmel complex if they had reasonably believed the children were going to be killed in a mass suicide. Attorney General Janet Reno has already admitted, however, that no such exigency existed on the day of the assault.

Government officials cannot use the color of their office to commit crimes against citizens. Since at least one child was struck by a ferret round, second degree murder charges may be appropriate. Note that such charges have been leveled against law enforcement officers after other controversial incidents. In 1999, for example, prosecutors in New York charged the police officers involved in the Amadou Diallo killing with "depraved indifference to human life," a second degree murder charge that carried a sentence of 25 years to life.

Whether or not sufficient proof can be mustered to sustain a second degree murder charge, charges relating to the reckless endangerment of human life are certainly in order.

FBI Agents Used Tanks to Demolish Sections of Mt. Carmel. The FBI has always admitted that its tear gas "insertion" plan called for tanks to smash holes in the walls of the Mt. Carmel complex. Government documents and testimony employ euphemisms to describe what happened. Reno, for example, referred to the tanks as "good rent-a-cars," and FBI supervisor Larry Potts spoke of "poking holes" in the building—as if nails, instead of tanks, were being driven into the walls of Mt. Carmel. Because federal officials and agents did not know where the Davidian children were located, it was both unconscionable and criminal to have the tanks smash into the residence and knock down walls.

Does anyone doubt that, if the Davidian adults had been holding children of senators and congressmen hostage within the Mt. Carmel buildings, the FBI's tank assault plan would have been rejected out of hand? Is it not equally clear that, if an ordinary citizen were to drive a car into the side of someone's home—indifferent to what might be on the other side of the wall—he would be prosecuted for second degree murder should someone be killed? The driver would also face lesser charges, such as reckless endangerment of human life.

The FBI's use of tanks on April 19, 1993, evinced an extreme indifference to human life. While it is unclear whether any Davidian was actually killed by the destructive activity of the tanks, the law pertaining to the reckless endangerment of human life was once again violated.

Conduct That Warrants Further Investigation

Whether the National Guard Helicopters Strafed Mt. Carmel. The Texas National Guard, the ATF, and the Department of Justice have always maintained that no one aboard the National Guard helicopters fired on the Davidians on February 28, 1993. The pilots and ATF field agents have all given sworn statements that no person fired on Mt. Carmel.

There is evidence to the contrary, however. Several Branch Davidians claim they received fire from the helicopters. Davidian Wayne Martin called 911 soon after the ATF arrived in a frantic attempt to end the gunfight. His recorded phone call includes a statement about shots from the helicopters. Federal officials have scoffed at the recorded statements, calling them "self-serving." (While that is possibly true, the same can be said about the denials from the ATF agents.)

Catherine Matteson, a 72-year-old Davidian, who was never accused of any crimes, told reporters that the helicopters fired on the residence. Another Davidian woman, Rita Riddle, told the *Los Angeles Times*, "I heard [the helicopters] spraying the building when they went over."

In a phone conversation recorded a few days after the initial raid, ATF agent Jim Cavanaugh tried to get David Koresh to acknowledge that the helicopters did not fire on

Mt. Carmel. When Koresh called the ATF agent a liar, Cavanaugh backed off and said he was not disputing the fact that there was fire from the helicopters, only that the helicopters did not have outside "mounted" guns, to which Koresh offered no objection.

The criminal defense attorneys who went into the residence during the siege saw bullet holes in the ceiling of Mt. Carmel with splinters of wood punched inward. The Davidians explained that those were some of the shots fired from the helicopters.

The FBI's use of tanks on April 19, 1993, evinced an extreme indifference to human life.

Special Prosecutor Danforth brushes all of those witnesses aside and concludes that there was no gunfire from the helicopters on February 28, 1993.

The ATF agents aboard the helicopters were supposed to divert the attention of the Davidians at the outset of the raid, film the raid as it unfolded, and, finally, transport the wounded (if any) to a nearby hospital. As the raid went awry, however, it is certainly plausible that the agents aboard the helicopters wanted to assist their fellow agents on the ground who were under heavy fire.

Understandable as that may be, National Guard regulations prohibit guard personnel from active participation in law enforcement activity. But if there was strafing of the roof of the Mt. Carmel residence, an even more serious allegation arises. Indiscriminate firing into the roof or walls of a building known to contain innocent people (e.g., children) could result in possible murder and reckless endangerment charges. Because of the conflicting testimony and the gravity of the allegations, further investigation of this matter is warranted.

Whether FBI Agents Knew about Any Davidian Fire Plan. FBI officials have always maintained that they had no prior knowledge of the Davidian plan to set fires. In testimony before Congress, Jeff Jamar, the FBI's on-scene commander at Waco, said: "If I knew about his plans to burn the place, we would have had another approach. . . . We would not even come close to approaching that place [e.g., the Branch Davidian residence]." Larry Potts, who was Jamar's supervisor in Washington, D.C., testified, "Any indication about danger to those children, the rule was—back off." The veracity of those high-ranking officials has now been directly challenged by a U.S. Army colonel who was at Mt. Carmel on April 19, 1993.

According to the *Dallas Morning News*, Col. Rodney L. Rawlings was assisting the FBI during the Waco siege. Rawlings told that newspaper that FBI "bugs" had been placed in Mt. Carmel during the standoff and that on April 19 he was present in an FBI monitoring room where the voices of the Davidians could be clearly heard. As the FBI tanks began to ram holes in Mt. Carmel, Rawlings said the bugging devices picked up the voices of David Koresh and his followers as they were preparing to start, and then starting, the fires.

Those audio recordings have been part of the public record for years. The FBI has used them in an effort to prove that the Davidians, not the bureau, started the fire. What is significant is that bureau officials have always maintained that the voices on the tapes were not clearly audible in "real time." The tapes had to be "enhanced" later to discover what was actually being said. Thus, the FBI did not have any advance warning of the Davidian fire plans.

Col. Rawlings, however, claimed that "you could hear everything from the very beginning, as it was happening." Rawlings further stated that FBI officials were "using the excuse of technical difficulties to cover why they didn't react to the information they had." When asked about the bureau's claim that it had no forewarning of the fire, Rawlings said, "That is the worst lie of all."

Colonel Rawlings appears to be a credible whistleblower. He is a combat-decorated helicopter pilot and a 31-year veteran who retired from the Army in 1997. Inexplicably, the Waco report prepared by Special Prosecutor John Danforth does not discuss Colonel Rawlings's allegations. If the FBI knew the Davidians were spreading fuel and making fire plans and did not stop the tanks from ramming the residence, murder, manslaughter, and perjury laws, among others, were violated.

Whether Gunfire Was Directed at the Davidians on April 19th. The FBI has always maintained that, throughout the entire siege, its agents never fired at the Branch Davidians. (The bureau does not deny firing the ferret rounds, however.) According to the FBI, the Davidians' gunshot wounds were either self-inflicted or inflicted by other Davidians.

Several infrared experts have come forward to contradict the FBI's claim, The FBI's aerial FLIR [Forward Looking Infrared, which detects heat] film from April 19, 1993, contains flashes of light. Edward Allard, a former employee of the Defense Department and a thermal imaging consultant for more than 30 years, appeared in the documentary film, *Waco: The Rules of Engagement*, and said those flashes were gunfire directed at Mt. Carmel. Maurice Cox, a retired intelligence analyst who worked on military satellite operations, appeared in the film, *Waco: A New Revelation*, and said the flashes of light were gunfire directed at Mt. Carmel. Carlos Ghigliotti, an expert in thermal imaging and videotape analysis who once did freelance work for the FBI, examined the FLIR tape and reached the same conclusion as Allard and Cox. Ghigliotti told the *Washington Post*, "The FBI fired shots that day." *60 Minutes* hired a British army expert in infrared imagery to examine the FLIR tape from April 19, 1993. That expert, Paul Weaver, said the flashes "look exactly as if they're gunfire."

Special Prosecutor John Danforth hired two experts to analyze the FLIR tape. They concluded that the flashes on the film were reflections off debris on the ground. Instead of acknowledging the conflicting expert testimony on this important issue and reporting that the evidence was inconclusive, Danforth proclaimed with "100 percent certainty" that the analyses performed by his experts showed that no gunfire was directed at the Davidians from government positions.

Ordinary citizens can use deadly force to defend themselves and others from imminent harm. But if someone fired a gun to keep others from fleeing a burning building, he would be subject to prosecution for murder. Because there is conflicting expert testimony as to what appears on the FLIR tapes, and because of the gravity of some of the experts' allegations, further investigation of this matter is warranted.

Whether Federal Employees Obstructed Justice. When Attorney General Janet Reno was asked in 1993 to identify those at the FBI who participated in the decisionmaking process regarding the April 19th assault plan, she mentioned, among others, (1) Assistant Director Larry Potts, (2) Deputy Assistant Director Danny Coulson, and (3) Michael Kahoe, chief of the FBI's Violent Crimes and Major Offenders Section. Those names should have set off alarm bells with Special Prosecutor Danforth's investigators.

Potts, Coulson, and Kahoe were suspended by the FBI in 1995 for their role in the controversial Ruby Ridge incident. Danforth does not mention that in his Waco report. The suspensions were not obscure personnel decisions. They were reported on the front pages of the *New York Times* and the *Washington Post*, among other newspapers.

[Senator John] Danforth's sweeping exoneration of federal officials is not supported by the factual record.

Kahoe was eventually sentenced to 18 months imprisonment for destroying evidence and lying to investigators about his role in the Ruby Ridge cover-up. He admitted boasting to his subordinates that, when Justice Department investigators asked him about his conduct in the affair, he gave them a bunch of "[expletive]." (That admission is itself a damning indictment of the FBI's internal culture.) Kahoe's defense attorney told the sentencing judge that Kahoe committed crimes to protect "what he wrongly perceived as the institutional best interest of the bureau." Department of Justice prosecutors told reporters that there was "insufficient evidence" to prosecute Potts and Coulson. Although FBI director Louis Freeh and the Department of Justice condemned Kahoe's crimes, they allowed him to remain on the federal payroll until he reached his 50th birthday—thus ensuring his eligibility for a federal pension. Potts and Coulson presumably received their pensions as well.

A serious probe into obstruction of justice by the bureau with respect to Waco would have quickly identified Potts, Coulson, and certainly Kahoe as potential suspects. Danforth should have hauled those individuals before a grand jury and questioned them about missing Waco evidence. He did not.

The FBI tactical commander at Waco, Richard Rogers, was also involved in the Ruby Ridge incident and was disciplined for his conduct there. When Congress sought to question him about his role at Ruby Ridge in 1995, Rogers declined to testify, citing his Fifth Amendment right against self-incrimination.

In the summer of 1999, previously undisclosed audio-tapes surfaced and revealed that Rogers actually gave the order to FBI field agents to fire pyrotechnic devices. That disclosure raised a deeply disturbing question: Why did Rogers sit passively behind Attorney General Reno when she gave sworn testimony to Congress in 1993 that py-rotechnic devices were not used against the Branch David-ians on April 19, 1993? When Danforth's investigators asked Rogers about the obvious discrepancy, Rogers said that he was not paying attention to Reno's testimony. Dan-forth chided Rogers for dereliction of duty but declined to prosecute him for "making or allowing others to make false or misleading statements." Danforth could have sent his dereliction of duty finding to the FBI and demanded disci-plinary action, including revocation of Rogers's pension. He did not. And FBI director Freeh, who tells Congress and the press that he takes any bureau controversy "with the most extreme seriousness," has not taken any action on his own against Rogers.

It is now clear that the FBI withheld relevant documents and videotapes from Congress, the Davidian lawyers, and citizens who filed Freedom of Information Act requests. The only question is whether that evidence was deliberately withheld or there was a series of bureaucratic "snafus." Spe-cial Prosecutor Danforth did not investigate the matter thoroughly. Obvious investigative leads were not followed. Indeed, with a convicted felon in a supervisory position on the Waco case, obstruction of justice seems not only possi-ble but probable. Further investigation into tampering and spoliation of evidence is warranted.

A Need for Answers

The Waco incident was the worst disaster in the history of federal law enforcement. More than 80 people (agents and civilians) lost their lives in 1993. The American people are entitled to know exactly what happened and why.

Unfortunately, the "official" investigation of the inci-dent, headed by former senator John Danforth, was soft and incomplete. Danforth's sweeping exoneration of federal of-ficials is not supported by the factual record.

It is certainly true that Branch Davidian leader David Koresh cannot escape his share of responsibility for the tragedy. Scores of lives could have been saved if he had simply walked out of Mt. Carmel and surrendered peacefully. But his refusal to do so cannot absolve federal officials from what they did at Waco.

Danforth hoped his report would help to restore the American people's "faith in government." After everything that has come to light in the years since the agents and the Davidians perished, it is difficult to follow Danforth's logic. The ATF, the FBI, and Attorney General Reno exploited the public's faith in government when they tried to deceive everyone about what happened in Waco. Recall, for example, that Reno had to recant her statement that "babies were being beaten" during the standoff.

Because numerous crimes at Waco have gone unpunished, the people serving in our federal police agencies may well come to the conclusion that it is permissible to recklessly endanger the lives of innocent people, lie to newspapers, obstruct congressional subpoenas, and give misleading testimony in our courtrooms. If such activity becomes more common than it is today, those agencies will surely become lawless and unaccountable. The only way to counter that danger is for the American people to *distrust* government officials, limit their powers, and demand accountability. In 1997 FBI director Louis Freeh told Congress, "We are potentially the most dangerous agency in the country if we are not scrutinized carefully." The carnage at Waco is grisly testament to that.

Chapter 3

Voices from Waco

1

A Call to 911

911 Transcript

At 9:48 A.M. on February 28, 1993, shortly after gunfire broke out between the Branch Davidians and the dozens of armed agents of the Bureau of Alcohol, Tobacco, and Firearms (BATF) who were attempting what is called a "dynamic entry," the phone rang at the local 911 dispatch center. The caller was Wayne Martin, a Branch Davidian and lawyer, and he reported that Mount Carmel was under attack. In the conversation, Martin insists that the Davidians were fired upon first, and he urges Lieutenant Larry Lynch of the sheriff's department to call off what he sees as an attack. According to Martin, the Davidians were defending themselves, and he pleads for a cease-fire. Approximately an hour later, the 911 tapes record a conversation between David Koresh and Lynch, in which Koresh condemns the BATF for their raid and begins to raise the kinds of theological issues that would characterize his many conversations with FBI negotiators in the weeks to come.

Female Dispatcher: 9-1-1. What's your emergency?

Martin: There are 75 men around our building shooting at us.

Dispatcher: OK. Just a moment.

Lynch: Hello. Hello. This is Lt. Lynch. May I help you?

Martin: Hello!

Lynch: Yeah. This is Lt. Lynch. May I help you?

Martin: Yeah. There are about 75 men around our building and they're shooting at us at Mt. Carmel.

Lynch: Mt. Carmel?

911 Transcript, "Excerpts from Transcript of Branch Davidian Calls to 911, February 28, 1993," www.carolmoore.net.

Martin: Yeah. Tell them there are women and children in here and to call it off!

Lynch: All right, all right. Hello? I hear gunfire [shots, rapid fire in background]. Oh, shit! Hello? Who is this? Hello.

Martin: Call it off! . . .

Lynch: Listen, calm down and talk to me for a minute, O.K.? Who is this? Calm down and talk to me. Who is this?

Martin: Wayne.

Lynch: Tell me what's happening, Wayne. This is Lynch at the sheriff's office. Tell me what's happening, Wayne? Talk to me, Wayne. Let's get this thing resolved, Wayne.

Martin: We got women and children in danger.

Lynch: O.K., Wayne, are there weapons in there with you, Wayne? Talk to me, Wayne, let's take care of the women and children, Wayne. Let's not do anything foolish we'll be sorry for. Talk to me, Wayne. I can't help you if you won't talk to me, Wayne.

Martin: Call it off!

Lynch: O.K., Wayne, work with me. Come to the phone and talk to me, Wayne. And let's settle this now before anybody gets hurt. Is anybody hurt in there, Wayne?

Martin: Yeah.

Lynch: Who's hurt?

Martin: I don't know, man screaming.

Lynch: What?

Martin: A man is screaming.

Lynch: O.K., Wayne, talk to me. Let's get this worked out. How many people are hurt, Wayne?

Martin: I'm under fire.

Lynch: O.K., Wayne, do you have weapons in there? Wayne, do you have weapons in there? Talk to me, Wayne, before this thing gets completely out of hand. Wayne, Wayne. Talk to me.

Martin: Tell them, cease fire!

Lynch: O.K. You ceased fire. Is that what you said, Wayne?

Maritn: No!

Lynch: Wayne, are there people injured in there?

Martin: Yes.

Lynch: Alright, Wayne, what we need you to do. What weapons do you have in there? You need to lay your weapons down and get some help for your people.

Martin: We're under fire.

Lynch: O.K. I'm fixing to get in touch with them, Wayne. Are you– We need you to lay your weapons down. Stand by while I make contact with the forces, O.K.? Are you injured, Wayne?

Martin: No. I'm under fire!

Lynch: O.K. I know you're under fire, but are you hurt?

Martin: Not yet!

Lynch: O.K. Wayne. Cease firing. Do not fire anymore. O.K.? Wayne, talk to me. Wayne, tell me how you are.

Martin: I have a right to defend myself. They started firing first.

Lynch: O.K. Let's resolve this, Wayne, before someone gets hurt. O.K.? I'm trying to make contact with the forces outside. O.K.?

Martin: O.K.!

We want to cease fire! We'll stop when they stop firing.

Lynch: I don't hear any gunfire, are you O.K.?

Martin: So far. . . . Someone is firing up there.

Lynch: Pardon me.

Martin: They're still attacking.

Lynch: Alright.

Unidentified Davidian: There's a chopper with more of them.

Lynch: What!?

Davidian: Another chopper with more people and more guns going off. Here they come!

Lynch: All right, Wayne, tell . . .

Davidian: We're not firing. That's not us, that's them.

Lynch: Are you, are you ready to come out and give up? Are you ready to terminate this, Wayne?

Martin: We want to cease fire! We'll stop when they stop firing. . . .

Lynch: [more shooting] Who's firing now?

Martin: They are!

Lynch: All right. Standby. I'm trying to reach them. Stand. Don't return fire, O.K.?

Davidian: We haven't been.

Lynch: What?

Davidian: We haven't been. . . .
Voices in background: Here they come! They coming.
Lynch: O.K. Are you returning fire, Wayne?
Martin: No.
Lynch: All right. Why are they shooting, Wayne?
Martin: Because that's them . . .
Lynch: What?
Martin: Oh, shit!
Lynch: What's the matter?
Martin: What do you think? They're doing all this firing at us right now. . . .
Lynch: O.K. We're working on it, so just hang, hang loose. Do not return fire, Wayne, O.K.? Just kind of hold what you've got 'til we get this situation settled and you're willing to talk to them?
Martin: Yeah.
Lynch: Will you visit with them?
Martin: Yeah!
Lynch: O.K. All right. We'll get you someone to talk to here in just a second.
Martin: Hello, Lynch?
Lynch: Yeah.
Martin: I gotta pass the word. . . .

A Second Call

Dispatcher: 9-1-1.
Koresh: Hello.
Dispatcher: Yes.
Koresh: This is David Koresh. We're being . . . Tough to call you guys.
Dispatcher: This is who, sir?
Koresh: David Koresh, Mt. Carmel Center. We're being shot all up out here.
Dispatcher: O.K. Where are you?
Koresh: Where am I? I'm at Mt. Carmel Center.
Dispatcher: O.K. Hang on just a second.
Koresh: All right.
Lynch: Yeah. This is Lynch.
Koresh: Hey, Lynch? That's a kind of funny name there.
Lynch: Ha! [surprised laugh] Now who am I speaking with?
Koresh: This is David Koresh.
Lynch: O.K., David.

Koresh: The notorious. What'd you guys do that for?

Lynch: What I'm doing is, I'm trying to establish some communications links with you.

Koresh: No. No. No. No. No. Let me tell you something.

Lynch: Yes, sir.

Koresh: You see, you brought a bunch of guys out here and you killed some of my children. We told you we wanted to talk. How come you guys try to be ATF agents? How come you try to be so big all the time?

Lynch: O.K., David.

Koresh: Now, there's a bunch of us dead. There's a bunch of you guys dead. Now, now, that's your fault.

Lynch: O.K. Let, let's try to resolve this now. Tell me this, now, you have casualties. How many casualties? Do you want to try to work something out? ATF is pulling back, we're trying to, ah . . .

Koresh: Why didn't you do that first?

Lynch: All I'm, all I'm doing is handling communications. I can't give you that answer, David.

Koresh: O.K.

Lynch: O.K.

Koresh: What is the deal? You pull your guys out. . . .

Lynch: I couldn't hear you. I've got Wayne on the other phone.

Koresh: Wayne Martin?

Lynch: Yes, he's on the other phone with me. I've been talking to him but you're the man I need to talk to, David.

Koresh: Well, let me tell you something. In our great country here the United States, you know God's given us a rich history of patronage, but we're not trying to be the bad guys.

Lynch: O.K.

Koresh: The thing of it is, is this. Look at the . . . I know it sounds crazy to you but . . .

Lynch: No, no.

Koresh: . . . You're gonna find out sooner or later.

Lynch: Sure. We all. . . .

Koresh: There are seven seals. The thing that theology has overstepped . . . not even opened the book. Now that's what I've done. Now, there's some things in that Bible that have been held as mysteries about Christ.

Lynch: Yes, sir.

Koresh: Now, when I'm told by the Theological Department that they are going to ruin me because of what I present out of the book just because they can't present it, and I can, there's a meaning to that.

Lynch: O.K.

Koresh: There are prophecies. . . .

Lynch: Let me. Can I interrupt you for a minute?

Koresh: Sure.

Lynch: All right. We can talk about theology, but right now . . .

Koresh: No. This is life. This is life and death.

Lynch: That's what I'm talking.

Koresh: Theology is life and death.

Lynch: Yes, sir. I agree with that.

Koresh: See. See. You have come and stepped on my perimeter.

Lynch: O.K.

Koresh: We will serve God first. Now, we will serve the God of the church. We're willing, and we've been willing, all this time, to sit down with anybody. You've sent law enforcement out here before.

Lynch: Yes, sir.

Koresh: And I've laid it straight across the table. I said, if you want to know about me, sit down with me and I'll open up a book and show you seven seals. Just like I told Robert. You know Robert, don't you? [Robert Rodriguez, the ATF undercover agent who infiltrated Mount Carmel.]

Lynch: Yes, sir.

Koresh: You know. The guy that . . . Your agent.

Lynch: Yes, sir.

Koresh: We've known about this. I've been teaching it for four years!

Lynch: O.K. Now . . .

Koresh: We, we knew you were coming and everything. You see . . .

Lynch: Yes, sir.

Koresh: . . . We knew before you even knew.

Lynch: Yes, sir.

Koresh: See, there is a spirit of prophecy; the testimony of Jesus Christ is a light that shines in a dark place. You need to learn Deuteronomy 32.

2

The Branch Davidians Were a Murderous Cult

Bill Clinton

On April 20, 1993, the day after the standoff at Waco ended with the deaths of most of those inside the building, President Bill Clinton held a press conference at which he gave his administration's view of events and fielded questions from reporters. In the following excerpts from those remarks, Clinton strongly defends the federal government's actions and directs his criticisms toward David Koresh, the leader of the Branch Davidians. According to Clinton, Koresh was an irrational and probably insane religious fanatic who broke both the law and common standards of decency. Furthermore, Clinton characterizes the Branch Davidians as a cult, describes their children as hostages and captives, and says that the cult members murdered each other and their children. Bill Clinton, a Democrat from Arkansas, was president from 1993 to 2001.

The President: On February the 28th [1993], four federal agents were killed in the line of duty trying to enforce the law against the Branch Davidian compound, which had illegally stockpiled weaponry and ammunition, and placed innocent children at risk. Because the BATF [Bureau of Alcohol, Tobacco and Firearms] operation had failed to meet its objective, a 51-day standoff ensued.

The Federal Bureau of Investigation then made every reasonable effort to bring this perilous situation to an end without bloodshed and further loss of life. The Bureau's ef-

Bill Clinton, "Remarks by the President in Question and Answer Session with the Press, April 20, 1993," http://clinton6.nara.gov, Office of the Press Secretary, White House, April 20, 1993.

forts were ultimately unavailing because the individual with whom they were dealing, David Koresh, was dangerous, irrational, and probably insane.

He engaged in numerous activities which violated both federal law and common standards of decency. He was, moreover, responsible for the deaths and injuries which occurred during the action against the compound in February. Given his inclination towards violence and in an effort to protect his young hostages, no provocative actions were taken for more than seven weeks by federal agents against the compound.

Koresh's response to the demands for his surrender by federal agents was to destroy himself and murder the children who were his captives, as well as all the other people who were there who did not survive.

This weekend I was briefed by Attorney General [Janet] Reno on an operation prepared by the FBI, designed to increase pressure on Koresh and persuade those in the compound to surrender peacefully. The plan included a decision to withhold the use of ammunition, even in the face of fire, and instead to use tear gas that would not cause permanent harm to health, but would, it was hoped, force the people in the compound to come outside and to surrender.

I was informed of the plan to end the siege. I discussed it with Attorney General Reno. I asked the questions I thought it was appropriate for me to ask. I then told her to do what she thought was right, and I take full responsibility for the implementation of the decision.

Yesterday's action ended in a horrible human tragedy. Mr. Koresh's response to the demands for his surrender by federal agents was to destroy himself and murder the children who were his captives, as well as all the other people who were there who did not survive. He killed those he controlled, and he bears ultimate responsibility for the carnage that ensued.

Now we must review the past with an eye towards the future. I have directed the United States Departments of Justice and Treasury to undertake a vigorous and thorough investigation to uncover what happened and why, and whether anything could have been done differently. I have told the departments to involve independent professional law enforcement officials in the investigation. I expect to receive analysis and answers in whatever time is required to complete the review. Finally, I have directed the departments to cooperate fully with all congressional inquiries so that we can continue to be fully accountable to the American people.

I want to express my appreciation to the Attorney General, to the Justice Department, and to the federal agents on the front lines who did the best job they could under deeply difficult circumstances.

Again, I want to say as I did yesterday, I am very sorry for the loss of life which occurred at the beginning and at the end of this tragedy in Waco. I hope very much that others who will be tempted to join cults and to become involved with people like David Koresh will be deterred by the horrible scenes they have seen over the last seven weeks. And I hope very much that the difficult situations which federal agents confronted there and which they will be doubtless required to confront in other contexts in the future will be somewhat better handled and better understood because of what has been learned now. . . .

The President Interviewed

Reporter: Can you describe what she [Attorney General Janet Reno] told you on Sunday [April 18, 1993] about the nature of the operation and how much detail you knew about it?

The President: Yes. I was told by the Attorney General that the FBI strongly felt that the time had come to take another step in trying to dislodge the people in the compound. And she described generally what the operation would be— that they wanted to go in and use tear gas which had been tested not to cause permanent damage to adults or to children, but which would make it very difficult for people to stay inside the building. And it was hoped that the tear gas would permit them to come outside.

I was further told that under no circumstances would our people fire any shots at them even if fired upon. They were going to shoot the tear gas from armored vehicles which would protect them and there would be no exchange of fire. In fact, as you know, an awful lot of shots were fired by the cult members at the federal officials. There were no shots coming back from the government side.

I asked a number of questions. The first question I asked is, why now? We have waited seven weeks; why now? The reasons I was given were the following:

Number one, that there was a limit to how long the federal authorities could maintain with their limited resources the quality and intensity of coverage by experts there. They might be needed in other parts of the country.

Number two, that the people who had reviewed this had never seen a case quite like this one before, and they were convinced that no progress had been made recently and no progress was going to be made through the normal means of getting Koresh and the other cult members to come out.

Number three, that the danger of their doing something to themselves or to others was likely to increase, not decrease, with the passage of time.

And number four, that they had reason to believe that the children who were still inside the compound were being abused significantly, as well as being forced to live in unsanitary and unsafe conditions.

So for those reasons, they wanted to move at that time. The second question I asked the Attorney General is whether they had given consideration to all of the things that could go wrong and evaluated them against what might happen that was good. She said that the FBI personnel on the scene and those working with them were convinced that the chances of bad things happening would only increase with the passage of time.

The third question I asked was, has the military been consulted? As soon as the initial tragedy came to light in Waco, that's the first thing I asked to be done, because it was obvious that this was not a typical law enforcement situation. Military people were then brought in, helped to analyze the situation and some of the problems that were presented by it. And so I asked if the military had been consulted. The Attorney General said that they had, and that they were in basic agreement that there was only one minor tactical difference of opinion between the FBI and the military—something that both sides thought was not of overwhelming significance.

Having asked those questions and gotten those answers, I said that if she thought it was the right thing to do, that she should proceed and that I would support it. And I stand by that today. . . .

Can you address the widespread perception—reported widely, television, radio and newspapers—that you were trying somehow to distance yourself from this disaster?

The President: No, I'm bewildered by it. The only reason I made no public statement yesterday—let me say—the only reason I made no public statement yesterday is that I had nothing to add to what was being said and I literally did not know until rather late in the day whether anybody was still alive other than those who had been actually seen and taken to the hospital or taken into custody. It was purely and simply a question of waiting for events to unfold. . . .

They were not just practicing their religion, they were—the Treasury Department believed that they had violated federal laws, any number of them.

I will say this, however. I was, frankly, surprised would be a mild word, to say that anyone that would suggest that the Attorney General should resign because some religious fanatics murdered themselves.

I regret what happened, but it is not possible in this life to control the behavior of others in every circumstance. These people killed four federal officials in the line of duty. They were heavily armed. They fired on federal officials yesterday repeatedly, and they were never fired back on. We did everything we could to avoid the loss of life. They made the decision to immolate themselves. And I regret it terribly, and I feel awful about the children.

But in the end, the last comment I had from Janet Reno, is when—and I talked to her on Sunday—I said, now, I want you to tell me once more why you believe—not why they believe—why you believe we should move now rather than wait some more. And she said, it's because of the children. They have evidence that those children are still being abused and that they're in increasingly unsafe conditions, and that they don't think it will get any easier with time—with the passage of time. I have to take their word for that. So that is where I think things stand.

Can we assume then that you don't think this was mishandled in view of the outcome, that you didn't run out of patience? And if you had it to do over again, would you really decide that way?

The President: No—well, I think what you can assume is just exactly what I announced today. This is a—the FBI has done a lot of things right for this country over a long period of time. This is the same FBI that found the people that bombed the World Trade Center [in 1993] in lickety-split, record time. We want an inquiry to analyze the steps along the way. Is there something else we should have known? Is there some other question they should have asked? Is there some other question I should have asked? Can I say for sure that no one—that we could have done nothing else to make the outcome come different? I don't know that. That's why I want the inquiry and that's why I would like to make sure that we have some independent law enforcement people, not political people, but totally non-political, outside experts who can bring to bear the best evidence we have.

There is, unfortunately, a rise in this sort of fanaticism all across the world. And we may have to confront it again. And I want to know whether there is anything we can do, particularly when there are children involved. But I do think it is important to recognize that the wrong-doers in this case were the people who killed others and then killed themselves. . . .

There are two questions I want to ask you. The first is, I think that they knew very well that the children did not have gas masks while the adults did, so the children had no chance because this gas was very—she said it was not lethal, but it was very dangerous to the children and they could not have survived without gas masks. And on February 28th [the day of the initial raid]—let's go back—didn't those people have a right to practice their religion?

The President: They were not just practicing their religion, they were—the Treasury Department believed that they had violated federal laws, any number of them.

What federal laws—

The President: Let me go back and answer—I can't answer the question about the gas masks, except to tell you that the whole purpose of using the tear gas was that it had been tested; they were convinced that it wouldn't kill either a child or an adult but it would force anybody that breathed it to run outside. And one of the things that I've heard—I don't want to get into the details of this because I don't know—but one of the things that they were speculating about today was that the wind was blowing so fast that the windows might have been opened and some of the gas might have escaped and that may be why it didn't have the desired effect.

They also knew, Sarah [the journalist to whom Clinton is speaking], that there was an underground compound—a bus buried underground where the children could be sent. And they were—I think they were hoping very much that if the children were not released immediately outside that the humane thing would be done and that the children would be sent someplace where they could be protected.

In terms of the gas masks themselves, I learned yesterday—I did not ask this fact question before—that the gas was supposed to stay active in the compound longer than the gas masks themselves were to work. So that it was thought that even if they all had gas masks, that eventually the gas would force them out in a nonviolent, nonshooting circumstance. . . .

Could you tell us whether or not you ever asked Janet Reno about the possibility of a mass suicide? And when you learned about the actual fire and explosion what went through your mind during those horrendous moments?

The President: What I asked Janet Reno is if they had considered all the worse things that could happen. And she said—and, of course, the whole issue of suicide had been raised in the public—he had—that had been debated anyway. And she said that the people who were most knowledgeable about these kinds of issues concluded that there was no greater risk of that now than there would be tomorrow or the next day or the day after that or at anytime in the future. That was the judgment they made. Whether they were right or wrong, of course, we will never know.

What happened when I saw the fire, when I saw the building burning? I was sick. I felt terrible. And my immediate concern was whether the children had gotten out and whether they were escaping or whether they were inside, trying to burn themselves up. That's the first thing I wanted to know.

3

We Were a Peaceful Religious Community

David Thibodeau

In the following piece, originally published in *Salon*, an online news magazine, David Thibodeau tells his version of the Waco story. Thibodeau was one of only nine Branch Davidians to survive the April 19, 1993, fire in which seventy-four Branch Davidians perished. Writing in 1999, six years after the stand-off, Thibodeau recounts his experience of that day and insists that the federal government has failed to be forthcoming in discussing its role in the siege and its tragic conclusion. He also tells the story of how he met David Koresh and came to be involved in the group. According to him, the Branch Davidians were a diverse, law-abiding group of people devoted to their religious faith, not a strange cult led by a madman. Thibodeau is the author, along with Leon Whiteson, of *A Place Called Waco: A Survivor's Story*.

A ttorney General Janet Reno says she's "very, very frustrated" over recent revelations that the FBI fired explosive devices at the Mount Carmel community outside of Waco, Texas, during the April 1993 siege. I know how Reno feels. I was one of only nine survivors of the Waco blaze—74 men, women and children died—and I've devoted the last six years to understanding what happened there. Frustration is a mild word to describe my feelings about that quest.

Reno's frustration, and mine, has only gotten worse recently as more damaging revelations have surfaced. First there was the CIA agent who told *Salon News* and the *Dal-*

las Morning News that members of the Army's secret Delta Force unit had actively participated in the siege. Then the FBI turned over tape recordings that include audio of an agent requesting and receiving permission to use pyrotechnic devices. Reports on Wednesday [Sept. 8, 1999] revealed the government also used incendiary flares during the Waco siege similar to those used to burn down the hideout of white supremacist Robert Matthews.

The film "Waco: The Rules of Engagement" purported to show infrared images of government agents firing on the building. Now there is also a rumored videotape, uncovered by the film's co-producer, Michael McNulty, that reportedly shows agents in an ATF helicopter shooting into Mount Carmel. No doubt there will be more evidence "discovered," more agents coming forward, their six-year amnesia about April 19 suddenly cured. The FBI has not come close to revealing the full government complicity in the Waco massacre.

Meeting Koresh

Obviously my stake is a bit more personal than most. Back in 1990 I had been drumming in a stagnant Los Angeles rock band when I met and befriended David Koresh. I needed some new drumsticks, and on the way to a gig stopped in at the Guitar Center on Sunset Boulevard.

Seeing the sticks in my hand, two strangers introduced themselves and asked if I was playing in a band. The two were David Koresh and Steve Schneider, the closest thing Koresh had to a deputy. Schneider gave me his card and I promptly handed it back. The backside was full of Bible verses. "You guys are a Christian band," I said, uninterested.

I had never been religious in my life, and though I sometimes found myself asking God for a little help, I couldn't remember the last time I had been in a church, let alone seriously prayed. But I did have a spiritual curiosity; there were questions—big questions—that I wanted answers to. Schneider and Koresh weren't pushy and made it clear that all they really were looking for right now was a drummer. "I'd like to play some music with you," Koresh said, "and see where we can go from there."

In truth, my band was going nowhere, and Koresh intrigued me. So I took the card back, and a few days later gave him a call. Over the next weeks I hung out with Koresh and some other musicians in his band. I got to know Koresh and was tremendously impressed. Having never paid much attention to the Bible, I was astonished to find that it actually did have some relevance to my life. And while Koresh had never gotten much in the way of formal education, it was clear that his knowledge of and insight into the scriptures was remarkable and profound.

Life in Waco

That fall I went out to Waco to play music and meet the larger community. I was pleasantly surprised by what I saw. The people at Mount Carmel were extremely involved in knowing and learning the Bible. In the process of demonizing Koresh and the Branch Davidians—a name we never used when describing ourselves—people have made it seem as if Mount Carmel came out of nowhere. In fact, Koresh was the third leader of a religious community that spun off from the Seventh Day Adventists in 1934. They had been living outside of Waco for almost 60 years before the ATF raid in 1993.

I was fascinated with their spiritual search, and I began—for the first time in my life—to read the Bible and to see that its message might be meaningful. Koresh was interesting, and the ways in which he explained the scriptures were complex and demanding. I didn't care that he wasn't a graduate of Yale divinity school. He was clearly a serious religious scholar and I wanted to understand what he was saying. So I stayed.

Koresh was interesting, and the ways in which he explained the scriptures were complex and demanding.

The people around Koresh came from many backgrounds. I met folks who hadn't finished high school, and others with degrees from places like Harvard law school. I spent time with African-Americans, Australians, black Britons, Mexican-Americans and more. One irony of the Waco disaster is that right-wing extremists and racists look to Mount Carmel as a beacon; if they realized that so many of us were black, Asian and Latino, and that we despised their hateful politics and anger, they would probably feel bitterly betrayed.

That isn't to say that all of us leaned to the left. We had some serious criticisms of the secular world that grew out of our faith. But we also had a "live and let live" attitude that had allowed the community to coexist with its Texas neighbors for all those decades. We certainly weren't as isolated as people seem to think. We shopped in town, some of us worked in the community and our band performed in Waco clubs. I worked as a bartender in Waco for a time and I doubt a single customer would tell you that I stood out in any way other than my ability to mix a mean margarita.

Government Dishonesty

Many have suggested that Koresh was a Jim Jones–like madman. But he wasn't. He had no plans for mass suicide; indeed, in sharp contrast to Jones, Koresh allowed members of the community to leave at any time, and many of them did, even during the siege. But many of us stayed, too, not because we had to, but because we wanted to. The FBI and ATF had been confrontational from the start, they had lied to us and they continued lying up through the siege.

The FBI and ATF had many pretexts for their attack on Mount Carmel. The initial ATF raid, in which four ATF agents and six Davidians were killed, was based on allegations that we were running a drug lab. But later even ATF employees would admit the charges were "a complete fabrication." One member had allowed speed dealers to operate from the building in the mid-1980s, but everyone knew Koresh hated drugs, and he'd asked the Waco sheriff to remove the methamphetamine lab when he took over as leader in 1987.

Charges that we were assembling an arsenal of weapons to be used against the government were equally off-base. We ran a business, buying and selling weapons at gun shows, to bring in revenue for the community. Only a few of us at Mount Carmel were directly involved with this—I personally had an aversion to guns—but it was a relatively profitable line of work. Everything was bought and sold on a legal basis. In fact, weeks before the raid, Koresh offered the ATF the opportunity to come out to Mount Carmel and inspect the building and every single weapon we had. They refused.

Maybe the most disturbing allegation, to those inside the building, was that we were engaging in child abuse there. The children of Mount Carmel were treasured, and they were a vital part of our small society. A disgruntled former resident, Marc Breault, was the original source of complaints about the treatment of children, and his wild allegations—that we were planning to sacrifice one of our children on Yom Kippur one year—were unfounded. Yes, occasionally kids were paddled for misbehaving, but the strict rule was they could never be paddled in anger. The parents usually did the paddling themselves. A few former residents also complained that David paddled their children, harshly, but I never saw that, and the Texas Child Protective Services workers who investigated the complaints concluded they were unfounded.

The biggest lie, though, is the FBI's claim that we set the building fire ourselves, to commit suicide. At the very least, the FBI has already provided proof that it created the conditions for a disaster. On the April morning when the FBI finally made its move, we had been under siege for 51 days. The FBI had cut off our power weeks earlier, so we had been resigned to heating the building with kerosene lamps. It was kerosene and gas from these lamps and the storage canisters, spilled over the floors as a result of collapsing walls and FBI munitions fire, that is often mistakenly taken as evidence that we doused Mount Carmel with an intent of burning it.

> *Truth is, we were desperate to live, to figure out a way to end the standoff. But the FBI, riled up, was not going to let that happen.*

Furthermore, the noxious CS gas that the FBI shot into Mount Carmel (almost 400 rounds were fired at us) was mixed with methylene chloride, which is flammable when mixed with air and can become explosive in confined spaces. CS gas is so nasty that the United States, along with 130 other countries, has signed the Chemical Weapons Convention banning its use in warfare. But apparently there is no prohibition against its use against American citizens.

The amount of gas the FBI shot into Mount Carmel was twice the density considered life threatening to an adult and even more dangerous for little children. Ironically, one of the questions that was asked of the FBI during the congressional hearings was "Why didn't you use an anesthetic gas that would have put the people inside to sleep?" The

FBI said it felt anesthetic gas would be harmful to the women and children.

No Suicide Pact

With powerful Texas winds whistling through the holes ripped in the building's sides and roof, Mount Carmel was primed to ignite. And while hours before the blaze FBI bugs inside Mount Carmel picked up, in the words of the *New York Times*, "ambiguous conversations" that seemed to be about setting the place on fire, I never heard any serious discussion of suicide or starting fires. I certainly never saw anyone try to do so. If we had really wanted to kill ourselves, we would not have waited 51 cold, hungry, scary days to do it. Truth is, we were desperate to live, to figure out a way to end the standoff. But the FBI, riled up, was not going to let that happen.

In fact, Koresh had negotiated a settlement to the crisis: He would leave peacefully, to be arrested and taken into custody by the Texas Rangers, as soon as he finished writing what he called his "Seven Seals" manuscript. David worked as fast as he could on this scriptural commentary, especially given the fact that he had been shot in the initial ATF raid and was struggling not only to write but simply to stay alive. The FBI thought the Seven Seals issue was just a ploy, and dismissed it. But it was legitimate, and in the ashes of Mount Carmel they found that Koresh had completed the first two commentaries and was hard at work on the third when the tanks rolled in.

It remains hard for me to clearly remember what happened after the tanks made their move. Walls collapsed, the building shook, gas billowed in and the air was full of terrible sounds: the hiss of gas, the shattering of windows, the bang of exploding rockets, the raw squeal of tank tracks. There were screams of children and the gasps and sobs of those who could not protect themselves from the noxious CS. This continued for hours. Inside Mount Carmel, the notion of leaving seemed insane; with tanks smashing through your walls and rockets smashing through the windows, our very human reaction was not to walk out but to find a safe corner and pray. As the tanks rolled in and began smashing holes in the building and spraying gas into the building, the FBI loudspeaker blared, "This is not an assault! This is not an assault!"

Around noon I heard someone yell, "Fire!" I thought first of the women and children, whom I had been separated from. I tried desperately to make my way to them, but it was impossible: rubble blocked off passageways, and the fire was spreading quickly. I dropped to my knees to pray, and the wall next to me erupted in flame. I smelled my singed hair and screamed. Community member Derek Lovelock, who had ended up in the same place as me, ran through a hole in the wall and I followed. Moments later, the building exploded.

Lingering Suspicions

In the years since the fire, I've tried desperately to find out what really happened. What I've discovered is disturbing. There is convincing evidence that the FBI did more than just create the conditions for a deadly inferno. The recent disclosures about the use of pyrotechnic weapons and incendiary flares show that they might have actually sparked the blaze. As almost any munitions expert will admit, the fuses on the sort of pyrotechnic devices the FBI now confesses to using are notoriously imprecise, and could quite possibly take as long as four or more hours before detonating.

And there are many other questions. A just released Defense Department document backs up the CIA agent's assertion that members of a classified U.S. Army Special Forces unit were present at the siege. According to U.S. law, the military is barred from domestic police work. Even more troubling is the fact that the unit members were, according to the document, warned explicitly "not to video the operation." Why?

Infrared images taken from surveillance planes seem to indicate that the FBI was—despite its denials—firing shots into the building and shooting at Branch Davidians who tried to flee. And while some experts dispute whether the infrared images contain proof of gunfire, there are also photographs that show one of the metal double-doors at the building's entrance riddled with what appear to be bullet indentations that could only have come from shooters outside Mount Carmel. Mysteriously, the FBI has said that this door totally disintegrated in the fire. Just as mysteriously, the adjacent door survived the fire in excellent condition. Tape recordings of the negotiations between the FBI and Koresh catch the government agents chronically lying about details big and small, almost as if they wanted the discussions to fail.

There are other questions: Why did the FBI call the local hospital hours before the siege and ask how many beds were available in its burn unit? Why did it not equip the tanks with a firefighting agent that would have put the flames out quickly? What did the FBI negotiator mean when he threateningly told us we "should buy some fire insurance"? Why did the FBI not allow anyone access to the crime scene for several hours, despite an agreement with the Texas Rangers that they would be allowed to inspect the area first? And on and on.

I often wonder why I survived the blaze while so many others did not. Perhaps it was to be some sort of a witness. That's why I wrote a book about the siege and Koresh and life at Mount Carmel. Maybe that's also why the recent Waco news has left me both angry and relieved. Angry because for so long the FBI has called others and myself liars for suggesting they did what they now admit they did. Relieved because perhaps the truth is finally, slowly, starting to emerge. The FBI lied about the pyrotechnic devices for six years, demonizing the Branch Davidians in the process. They also inspired a large number of extremists—people like Timothy McVeigh—who in turn have killed others, even though we had no affinity with the right.

What's harder to believe: that the FBI, by shooting explosive devices into an area they had saturated with flammable gas, helped spark a deadly inferno? Or that the FBI honestly didn't know anything at all about the evidence that it has suddenly discovered in its files and recollections? Let us hope that we do not have to wait another six years before the complete and terrible truth about what happened on that cold April morning is finally disclosed.

4

The FBI and the Local Sheriff Remember Waco

Jeff Jamar, Clint Van Zandt,
Barry Higginbotham, and Jack Harwell

In 1995, the PBS show *Frontline* produced *Waco: The Inside Story*. Below are excerpts from interviews *Frontline* conducted with three FBI agents who played a major role in Waco and with Jack Harwell, the local sheriff. The four reflect on the standoff and share their impressions of the events and persons involved. First, Jeff Jamar, who was the FBI Special Agent in Charge and site commander, describes the FBI's motives for bringing heavy military equipment to the scene. Next, Special Agent Clint Van Zandt, who was a chief negotiator at Waco, remembers his conversations with David Koresh during the standoff. Following him, Barry Higginbotham, who was a member of the FBI hostage rescue team, tells what it was like to be at the front lines, with the tactical squad. Finally, the local sheriff, Jack Harwell, remembers his encounters over the years with David Koresh and the rest of the Branch Davidians.

Special Agent in Charge Jeff Jamar

Why did you use the Bradleys?
Jamar: The Bradleys are armored vehicles. They're called Bradley fighting vehicles. Of course we had all the firepower removed. There were no cannons or anything on them. We used them for transportation. And they're more than a personnel carrier—they're a track vehicle. I mean it's mud, just thick mud there the whole time. And the agents learned how to drive 'em. But the idea was to protect them as

Jeff Jamar, Clint Van Zandt, Barry Higginbotham, and Jack Harwell, "'Waco: The Inside Story. Who's Who.' Interview Excerpts," www.pbs.org, *Frontline*, 1995. Copyright © 1995 by WGBH/Boston. Reproduced by permission.

best we could. And we didn't know—they talked about blowing a 50—did they have rockets? Who knows? Did they have explosives buried in various vicinities? Are they prepared to run out with Molotov cocktails? What's in their mind?

So when he (Koresh) said we'll blow those (Bradleys)—this is several days into the event, I started asking: What can we bring in, so we can still get around? Let's say that something happens to a Bradley, what can we bring in that can withstand most of what they might have? And so the Abrams [tanks] were brought in. That's why—when we were going to ask for the Abrams, I'm thinking—I started asking: Isn't there something we can use like a truck, a tractor or a bulldozer? And they said, yeah, they got these CEV's [Combat Engineering Vehicles]. And they're tanks, you know, chassis armored with a blade on them. And then we ended up getting a couple of those. We got more of them later.

And we had these breakdowns with them. And so we got these pullers. You know, this M-80, M-88 [the M-88 is an armored recovery vehicle], it was a thing to tow those things. Because they're throwing tracks [the tracks were coming off] in the mud and everything and it was really frustrating. But we decided that we needed to show them that maybe you think you can go blow up the Bradleys, but that's not going to be enough for you because we've got this too.

And that's what this was about. It was more to say: We're not going away; we're not going to sit still to let you do what you will to our people here. But again, no firepower. And we told them that. That's the other thing I want to get across, more than anything else: We didn't do anything without telling them first. Like: We're going to come on, we're going to be going to this house across the street; we're going to be doing this. If you listen to the tapes, we told them everything we did. So there was no surprises. We didn't want to provoke anything. . . .

FBI Negotiator Clint Van Zandt

[On conversations with Koresh]

Van Zandt: Koresh was so adept at talking to his quote unquote congregation. As you know, he'd talk to them for six, twelve, eighteen hours. He wouldn't let them use the bathroom facilities. He'd keep everybody standing, so Koresh was used to holding a crowd and dominating. One of the things Koresh did, 'cause I spoke to him three hours one night, and he really tries to over-talk you. He would try to over-talk you, he would try to talk, sometimes, louder, or he would try—you listen to the tapes—and sometimes he would not take a breath. I mean, he would just, boom, boom, boom, boom, boom, boom, boom, move along, and he would attempt to break your train of thought and just dominate the conversation. While the negotiators, again, their job would be to try to break that. If that's what Koresh was comfortable in, dah dah-dah, dah dah-dah, dah dah-dah, break that—cut that off into bites, OK? But, David, let's talk about this. And get him on an issue, ah, other than what he wanted to talk about, which was always Revelation.

Dozens and dozens of letters came every day with Americans saying any where from why don't you bomb the place and quit screwing around, to why don't you go away and leave those people alone.

Why weren't [biblical scholars Phillip] Arnold and [James] Tabor used in negotiating with Koresh? They claimed they made a religious connection to him?

Van Zandt: I think you've got to draw the line someplace as to how do we not make this a circus event, how do we not have so many people talking and then going out and making public statements and then having it come back in via the radio. I mean, you try what seems logical and what seems best without totally abdicating your responsibilities, which for us was to negotiate. And I think we talked about the one time. I read every letter that came. The American public was sending letters. Dozens and dozens of letters came every day with Americans saying any where from why don't you bomb the place and quit screwing around, to why don't you go away and leave those people alone. And easily, 6, 8, 10, 12 letters would come in, and I read every one of them every day. One time a letter came in, and some good citizen said, the word might be Beelzebub, or hypothetical, I forget what the word was, but he said, this is a code word to David Koresh.

If you say this word, everybody's going to come out. I read this letter, and I thought, naw. I took a 3 × 5 card, and

I wrote on it, use the word "x" in your conversation with Koresh. And I walked into the negotiator who was on the phone, and I slid it in front of him. And I see this look on his face like—"what?" I said, do it. So he went ahead and did it. I sat there and waited for Koresh to come walking out. Did I think he would? No. Did I think it was worth the try? Anything was worth a try to even go to those extremes. Everybody was volunteering to come and talk with them— I'm a pastor. . . I'm also Christ incarnate. We've got all of those suggestions from people. Now, I don't place Arnold in the same ballpark as I do some good but maybe deranged person writing in. I think they had all the academic and professional credentials. But again, that would have been the Mickey Mantle and Koresh just hitting off of two major league pitchers. I don't think they would have been the ones. They didn't have the magic bullet or the magic hook that was going to bring Koresh out.

How do you know?

Van Zandt: How do I know? I would only know if we turned the clock back and let them try. OK? And then let everybody else try who wanted to try also. You know, we could have sold tickets and lined up 1,000 people. Who wants to negotiate with David Koresh? Come on in. . . .

When did you know they weren't coming out?

Van Zandt: When I saw the building come down on top of them and nobody came out.

What was your thinking at that moment?

Van Zandt: What an absolute classic tragedy. What a total indictment almost of mankind's inability to communicate and relate, even though we have different religious or personal philosophies, that this is how wars start, because people can't communicate and don't or won't understand each other, and that this was simply a microcosm of every conflict that man has ever had. . . .

FBI Hostage Rescue Team Member Barry Higginbotham

Did you understand what the negotiators were getting, or are you out there just watching it?

Higginbotham: I think we'd get about half of what was going on usually. Those of us on the front lines. Through whoever's fault that was. Just how it was disseminated down to the front lines.

But I remember the moment where they brought the buses up, and those of us that were in my position were just looking at each other and said, "We know they're not going to come out, why are they doing this?" And they certainly did not come out. And afterward we just all looked at each other, said, "This was no surprise to us, we know they're not going to come out of there."

We just felt that if you make them suffer a little more, deny them perhaps a little more food, lighting, power, things like that inside, that would cause more pressure on their leadership inside.

How did you know?

Higginbotham: Basically, a gut feeling. As a sniper observer, our whole team there, we were the eyes of the entire operation—we are the negotiators' eyes. They're all the way in the rear. They're talking to Koresh on the phone but they don't get to see his day-to-day activity, his body motions, the motions of his sentries as how they even change posts at the doors. We see how alert they are, we see how they're cleaning their weapons up in the windows, watching us.

And when a person's cleaning their weapons and stacking their ammunition and we're watching that, we're relaying that back, we know they're not getting ready to come out on a bus and give up. And that's why in a way we just looked at each other and said, "We could have told them that," that they're not coming out. Not at this moment at least.

What about the analyses of those who said the tighter you get, the more you're going to drive them together—the more you're going to play into their Armageddon sort of mindset?

Higginbotham: I can only go by my observations each day on the front. As I say, the sniper observers, they were the eyes of the operation. When you see something visually each day, their activity inside, how much freedom and leisure they have inside, how they even have recreation perhaps. They're sitting on guard posts reading and all. Things are not that bad inside then. And to me, you need to make them a little more hazardous inside. And tighten 'em down a little bit. Make them not as comfortable. Let them be cold for a while. Deny them food, deny them water. And let them go to their leadership inside, and let them deal with that pressure. And I think that would cause better negotiations.

What is your view of the decision making of those in charge?

Higginbotham: The leadership of the tactical forces and negotiators, and the overall on-scene command, they all had a very difficult job. It was a very hard balance to weigh the security of the tactical forces against that of the children and others inside the compound. And how they might suffer as a result of any action we took. Overall I felt the commanders had to always consider our security the most important thing. And I think they made very good decisions. And the negotiators did a wonderful job.

I think this whole situation does not fit into any kind of negotiation scenario that's ever been developed or they've had to deal with. Especially because of the duration of it. And it got down to, toward the end, no matter what they did, nothing worked. The progress stopped. And those of us up front could see that a lot sooner than they could back in the rear, 10 or 12 miles away, in a sterile atmosphere, where they're just receiving phone calls.

I think if they had been able to physically see it more up front, they would have seen that this is not going to work. He's not going to give in. They're too comfortable. There's no real hardships inside. They're not suffering. We just felt that if you make them suffer a little more, deny them perhaps a little more food, lighting, power, things like that inside, that would cause more pressure on their leadership inside. And perhaps their leadership would go to Koresh and pressure him to start negotiating in good faith. It was hard to believe that Koresh was ever negotiating in good faith. . . .

Local Sheriff Jack Harwell

You knew them. Who was Vernon Howell [as David Koresh was originally named]? Who was Steve Schneider? [Koresh's major liaison with the FBI]

Harwell: Steve Schneider had a degree in theology. Wayne Martin, I'd seen quite often here in the courthouse. He was an attorney. We weren't dealing with a bunch of uneducated people. For instance, Wayne Martin was recognized here as a good attorney. I don't know about all the people out there, but I know that there were some well-educated people there who, because of their religion, maybe were different, but otherwise, they were just normal, everyday good people. . . .

What was your take on him [Vernon Howard, as David Koresh was previously known]?

Harwell: When I talked to Vernon, he was always levelheaded, seemed nice, he was always courteous. He'd invite us out to his place to fish in his lake out there. The times that my people went out to the place on calls that we had out there, they were always courteous and I think he invited some of the other deputies who work for me out there to fish with him, and just come out and visit. . . .

It's kind of a frustrating thing to think about. Here are people out there, and you know that most of them want to live, they're enjoying life. Those who I'd come into contact with seemed to be good people.

This was a man who had everything he wanted inside that place out there, and nothing he wanted on the outside other than the freedom to come and go as he wanted to, but, "Leave me alone. I'm in my little country out here. I'm not in this country, and I don't want anyone coming out here interfering with what we're doing." And that's kind of the way he wanted things. It was the way I saw it.

It's kind of a frustrating thing to think about. Here are people out there, and you know that most of them want to live, they're enjoying life. Those who I'd come into contact with seemed to be good people. Some of them worked in various areas here in the community, and one of them was the mail carrier, as has been publicized. And then, to have this kind of thing happen, it's kind of frustrating.

Can you speak to the criticism that some people have for some of the FBI people involved?

Harwell: I've been in law enforcement over 32 years, and there's many things you do that you're going to get criticized for. The criticism that has been directed toward the FBI, ATF, all the people involved out there—it's easy to sit and say, "Well, they shouldn't have done this."

They were all well intended and they didn't want the outcome of this to be what it was any more than anyone else did. I can only praise all the people who were out there working. They really did everything they could, or that they thought was right to resolve this thing in a peaceful way. Until the last time that I heard them talking they were still working every angle they could, trying to get the thing resolved. They were very professional. The only thing I can say is that sometimes professionalism gets in your way. Rules and regulations.

Not to criticize anyone, but you need to let some common sense, some good ole' horse sense get mixed in there somewhere. It's like going out on a family disturbance. You can't set down a set of rules that you go by when you go out on a family disturbance, and not to say that there's any comparison between the two, but you're trained to do certain things. That training can only carry you so far. Then you have to get the feel of a situation, a feel of people, not "I'm a negotiator dealing with people." "I'm a human being dealing with another human being."

So let's get the rules and regulations out of the way and let's get down and talk where we can understand each other and show that we care for each other. We care what's going to happen, and I care about what's going to happen about you.

That's why I didn't fear them shooting me, or any of the other agents out there, unless there was some provocation to do it, because even though they had a religious belief that I don't agree with, maybe, or others don't agree with, but their religion didn't teach them to go out there—I'm not talking about Vernon Howell now because I'm talking about the people. That didn't teach them to go out here and shoot other people or do harm to other people. They hadn't done that to any of their community out there, the neighbors.

Chronology

June 4, 1992
Acting on a tip, the Bureau of Alcohol, Tobacco, and Firearms (BATF) starts investigating the Branch Davidians on the suspicion that they are illegally manufacturing weapons at Mount Carmel, a seventy-seven acre ranch and religious center near Waco, Texas.

February 25, 1993
The BATF asks for and receives warrants to search Mount Carmel and arrest David Koresh, the group's leader.

February 28, 1993
Shortly after 9 A.M., over seventy agents of the BATF stage a "dynamic entry" in an attempt to serve a search warrant on Mount Carmel and arrest David Koresh. Gunfire breaks out and four federal agents are killed, sixteen are wounded, and an unknown number of Davidians are killed and wounded. The FBI takes over and sets up a Hostage Rescue Team and a negotiating team. In telephone conversation, Koresh reveals that he has been wounded in the hip and left wrist. CNN interviews him over the phone and Dallas radio station KRLD agrees to broadcast his religious teachings. Michael Schroeder, a Branch Davidian coming home from work, is shot and killed by BATF agents as he approaches Mount Carmel. The Texas Rangers begin an investigation but the FBI bars them from continuing.

March 1, 1993
Hostage negotiations continue and over the course of the day, ten children are sent out of the center. The FBI positions agents in armored vehicles around the perimeter of Mount Carmel and cuts the phone line to permit calls only to negotiators. At least twice, Koresh says suicide is not being considered. FBI director William Sessions and President Bill Clinton agree on a "waiting strategy."

March 2, 1993
Koresh makes a one-hour tape of his teachings and promises to surrender if the tape is broadcast nationally.

The Christian Broadcasting Network broadcasts the tape at 1:30 P.M. At 6 P.M., Koresh says that God has told him not to surrender, but to wait.

March 3–4, 1993
Negotiations continue, with Koresh often focusing on theological issues. FBI psychological profilers Pete Smerick and Mark Young say a strategy of negotiations and increasing tactical pressure could be counterproductive.

March 5, 1993
Nine-year-old Heather Jones leaves Mount Carmel. A note pinned to her jacket, written by her mother, says that once the children are out the adults will die. Koresh denies suicide is an option.

March 6, 1993
Steve Schneider, who works closely with Koresh, suggests that federal agents might burn down the center in order to get rid of evidence. Schneider and Koresh are agitated and upset for most of the day.

March 7, 1993
Smerick and Young advise against tactical options and recommend instead that negotiators establish trust with Koresh.

March 8, 1993
The Davidians send a videotape of the children out of the center. The FBI does not release the tape to the media, as it is concerned that doing so would generate sympathy for Koresh.

March 9, 1993
In the middle of the night, Mount Carmel's electricity is cut off. Koresh refuses to speak to negotiators until it is restored. Schneider is outraged that armored vehicles are moving around the center. Members of the Hostage Rescue Team see weapons in the windows.

March 12, 1993
Janet Reno is sworn in as attorney general. Kathy Schroeder leaves Mount Carmel, saying suicide is not being contemplated. Jeff Jamar, the FBI commander on the scene, orders the electricity cut off for good, over the objections of FBI negotiators. The Davidians say the power shutoff is a "huge, huge setback."

March 13, 1993
Schneider is upset, and says that people inside Mount Carmel are getting very cold.

March 14, 1993
The FBI shines bright lights on Mount Carmel at night in order to disrupt the sleep of the Branch Davidians.

March 15, 1993
The FBI changes its negotiating strategy, refusing to listen to any more of what it calls "Bible babble." The BATF orders its agents in Waco not to discuss the February 28 raid in public.

March 18, 1993
In a message broadcast over loudspeakers, the FBI promises Branch Davidians that they will be treated fairly if they leave Mount Carmel.

March 19, 1993
Two Davidians, Brad Branch and Kevin Whitecliff, leave Mount Carmel.

March 20–21, 1993
Rita Riddle, Gladys Ottman, Sheila Martin, James Lawton, and Ofelia Santoya leave Mount Carmel. On the evening of March 21, the FBI starts playing disruptive and annoying music over loudspeakers. Koresh says, "Because of the loud music, nobody is coming out."

March 22, 1993
FBI negotiators attempt to placate Schneider, who is angry about the loud music, by blaming FBI tactical agents. The FBI Crisis Management Team meets to discuss "stress escalation measures."

March 23, 1993
Livingstone Fagan leaves Mount Carmel. He is the last Davidian to leave during the standoff. Assistant U.S. Attorney William Johnston of Waco writes Reno to complain about how the FBI is handling the standoff. That night, the FBI shines floodlights on Mount Carmel and broadcasts tapes of the negotiations and messages from Davidians outside Mount Carmel.

March 24, 1993
In the middle of the night, the FBI broadcasts Tibetan chants, Christmas music, and other sounds. Schneider refuses to talk, citing his anger at the noise. At a morning news conference, the FBI calls Koresh a liar and a coward.

March 25, 1993
The FBI announces that ten to twenty people must leave Mount Carmel by 4 P.M. At 4 P.M., armored vehicles move close to the center and remove motorcycles and go-carts.

March 26, 1993
Lights and music, as well as helicopter activity, continue throughout the night. After another ultimatum, armored vehicles clear part of the yard.

March 28, 1993
Koresh says that he has no intention of dying and that he is waiting for word from God. A videotape sent out from Mount Carmel shows nineteen children looking healthy.

March 29, 1993
The FBI permits a face-to-face meeting in the door of Mount Carmel between David Koresh and Dick DeGuerin, an attorney representing him. The meeting lasts nearly two hours.

March 30, 1993
Koresh and DeGuerin meet twice more.

March 31, 1993
The deputy assistant attorney general, Mark Richard, holds meetings to look into reports of infighting among the officials in Waco.

April 1, 1993
After spending the day inside Mount Carmel, DeGuerin tells the FBI the Davidians will surrender on either April 2 or April 10, depending on how they observe Passover. The religious scholars James D. Tabor and Phillip Arnold appear on talk radio, discussing an interpretation of the Book of Revelation that is an alternative to Koresh's interpretation.

April 5, 1993
The Davidians observe Passover.

April 6, 1993
The FBI broadcasts music throughout the night.

April 9, 1993

Koresh sends a letter to the FBI (followed by several others in the coming days). Experts suggest he is psychotic and has no intention of leaving Mount Carmel.

April 10, 1993

The FBI surrounds Mount Carmel with concertina wire (spiral barbed wire).

April 12, 1993

FBI director William Sessions, along with other high-ranking Justice Department and FBI officials, present the tear gas plan to Reno. Her initial reaction is to ask repeatedly, "Why now? Why not wait?" They convince her action is needed.

April 13, 1993

Associate Attorney General Webster Hubbell meets with Bill Clinton's aides to discuss the CS gas plan. Hubbell approves of FBI's plan. White House counsel Bernard Nussbaum tells Clinton that the handling of Waco is the jurisdiction of the Justice Department.

April 14, 1993

Koresh says he will surrender after he has had a chance to write down his interpretation of the Seven Seals. Harry Salem, an army doctor, and two military experts meet with Reno and tell her what is known about the effect of CS gas on children ("although there had been no laboratory tests performed on children relative to the effects of the gas, anecdotal evidence was convincing that there would be no permanent injury"). FBI tells Reno food and water supplies at Mount Carmel could last one year.

April 15, 1993

The FBI's chief negotiator at Waco, Byron Sage, has a two-hour phone conversation with Hubbell. Hubbell becomes convinced that negotiators believe negotiation with Koresh is futile.

April 16, 1993

Koresh says he has finished writing down his interpretation of the First Seal.

April 17, 1993

Reno meets with Hubbell, Sessions, and other top Justice Department officials and approves the tear gas plan.

April 18, 1993
Reno briefs Clinton on the CS gas plan. He asks about the safety of the children but tells her it is her decision. Armored vehicles remove Davidian vehicles from in front of Mount Carmel.

April 19, 1993
At 6 A.M., Sage phones the Davidians and tells them about the tear gas plan. Over a loudspeaker, Sage tells Davidians they are under arrest and should surrender peacefully. Two FBI Combat Engineer Vehicles spray gas into Mount Carmel. The Davidians respond with gunfire. The FBI shoots ferret rounds (tear gas) through the windows. At 6:30, the FBI reports the whole building is being gassed. At 7:30, one of the armored vehicles breaches the front side of the building while injecting gas. The FBI orders more gas from Houston and forty-eight ferret rounds arrive by 9:30 A.M. Around 9:30, two of the armored vehicles rip holes into the side of the building, apparently to create holes from which Davidians could leave. Shortly before noon, a wall on the right-hand side, near where one of the armored vehicles had been breaching the compound, collapses. Just after noon, fire breaks out. Nine Davidians escape and are arrested. Around 12:30 P.M., there is the sound of gunfire in the center. Mount Carmel burns to the ground. Seventy-six Branch Davidians die, mostly from smoke inhalation. Twenty have gunshot wounds. At a press conference, Reno says that the government was moved to action because of reports that "babies were being beaten." She acknowledges the plan was a failure and offers her resignation to President Bill Clinton, who refuses to accept it.

April 28, 1993
The Judiciary Committee of the House of Representatives holds a one-day hearing, at which Reno admits she has no evidence that any child was beaten at any time during the standoff.

May 23, 1993
60 Minutes rebroadcasts its January show on sexual harassment within the BATF. Mike Wallace says that almost all the BATF agents he spoke to report that the February 28 raid on Mount Carmel was a publicity stunt.

October 1, 1993
The Treasury Department (which is responsible for the BATF) issues its report on Waco. It is critical of senior agents at the bureau, saying they tried to deceive Congress and investigators. Shortly thereafter, the head of the Treasury Department announces he is replacing the head of the BATF and suspending five agents.

October 8, 1993
The Justice Department issues its report on Waco, which praises the FBI.

February 26, 1994
Five Branch Davidians are found guilty of voluntary manslaughter. Eleven are acquitted of murder and conspiracy to commit murder. The *New York Times* calls the verdicts "a stunning defeat not only for the Justice Department, but for the Bureau of Alcohol, Tobacco, and Firearms." Reno says the verdicts vindicate the government's version of events.

April 19, 1995
Exactly two years after the final fire at Mount Carmel, Timothy McVeigh bombs a federal building in Oklahoma, killing 168. Although McVeigh has no connection to the Branch Davidians, in a letter written later he explains he was motivated by anger at what happened at Waco: "I reached the decision to go on the offensive—to put a check on government abuse of power."

July 19, 1995
The House holds a ten-day hearing to investigate what went wrong at Waco.

July 11, 1996
A congressional report says Reno was negligent in authorizing the final FBI assault.

July 28, 1999
The *Dallas Morning News* reports that the Texas Rangers have discovered evidence that the FBI may have used pyrotechnic devices at Waco, something it has denied for six years.

August 25, 1999
The FBI admits that some pyrotechnic rounds were used on April 19, 1993. It insists, however, that they did not cause the fire.

August 30, 1999
William Johnson, the federal prosecutor in Waco, sends a letter to Reno, saying "I have formed the belief that facts may have been kept from you—and quite possibly are being kept from you even now, by components of the Department [of Justice]."

September 9, 1999
Reno appoints former U.S. senator John Danforth to lead an investigation into the standoff.

September 15, 1999
The Justice Department removes Johnson, the federal prosecutor, from the Waco case.

June 18, 2000
The surviving Branch Davidians' wrongful death suit against the government begins.

July 14, 2000
The jury in the wrongful death suit finds federal officials are not responsible for the deaths of the Davidians in 1993.

September 21, 2000
A U.S. district judge rules that the government is not to blame for the deaths of those Branch Davidians who died in the final 1993 fire.

July 21, 2000
Danforth releases an interim report, which largely exonerates the government.

November 8, 2000
Danforth gets a grand jury indictment of former federal prosecutor Bill Johnson, whom he accuses of having concealed his knowledge that the FBI used pyrotechnic devices at Waco. Johnson says he is being scapegoated because he alerted Reno to the possibility of a cover-up.

February 6, 2001
Johnson pleads guilty to a single charge of obstructing the investigation into the Waco standoff. In return, Danforth drops five other felony charges and recommends probation.

For Further Research

Books

Jack De Vault, *The Waco Whitewash*. San Antonio, TX: Rescue Press, 1994.

Ken Fawcett, *Blind Justice: A Chronology of the Historic Trial of Eleven Branch Davidians in January 1994*. Royse City, TX: Electropress, 1994.

Mark S. Hamm, *Apocalypse in Oklahoma: Waco and Ruby Ridge Revenged*. Boston: Northeastern University Press, 1997.

Anthony A. Hibbert, *Before the Flames: David Koresh and the Branch Davidians*. Long Island, NY: Seaburn Press, 1996.

David B. Kopel and Paul H. Blackman, *No More Wacos: What's Wrong with Federal Law Enforcement and How to Fix It*. Amherst, NY: Prometheus Books, 1997.

David Koresh, *The Decoded Message of the Seven Seals of the Book of Revelation*. Green Forest, AR: Stewart Waterhouse, 1993.

James R. Lewis, ed., *From the Ashes: Making Sense of Waco*. Lanham, MD: Rowman and Littlefield, 1993.

Carol Moore, *The Davidian Massacre*. Franklin, TN: Legacy Communications, 1995.

Dick J. Reavis, *The Ashes of Waco: An Investigation*. New York: Simon and Schuster, 1995.

James D. Tabor and Eugene V. Gallagher, *Why Waco? Cults and the Battle for Religious Freedom in America*. Berkeley: University of California Press, 1995.

Stuart A. Wright, ed., *Armageddon in Waco: Critical Perspectives on the Branch Davidian Conflict*. Chicago: University of Chicago Press, 1995.

Periodicals

Gary Benoit, "The Last Word: The FBI Admits It Lied," *New American*, October 11, 1999.

Paul S. Boyer, "A Brief History of the End of Time: The American Roots of the Branch Davidians," *New Republic*, May 17, 1993.

Peter Boyer, "Children of Waco," *New Yorker*, May 15, 1995.

William Norman Grigg, "Waco Deception Up in Smoke," *New American*, September 27, 1999.

Newsweek, "The Secrets of David Koresh's Waco Cult," March 15, 1993.

Joe Rosenbloom III, "Waco: More than Simple Blunders?" *Wall Street Journal*, October 17, 1995.

Official Documents and Reports

Report of the Department of the Treasury on the Bureau of Alcohol, Tobacco, and Firearms Investigation of Vernon Wayne Howell, also Known as David Koresh. Washington, DC: U.S. Government Printing Office, 1993.

U.S. Department of Justice, *Evaluation of the Handling of the Branch Davidian Stand-off in Waco, Texas*. Washington, DC: U.S. Government Printing Office, 1993.

U.S. Department of Justice, *Recommendations of Experts for Improvements in Federal Law Enforcement After Waco*. Washington, DC: U.S. Government Printing Office, 1993.

U.S. Department of Justice, *Report to the Deputy Attorney General on the Events at Waco, Texas, February 28 to April 19, 1993*. Washington, DC: U.S. Government Printing Office, 1993.

U.S. House Committee on Government Reform, *The Tragedy at Waco: New Evidence Examined: Eleventh Report*. Washington, DC: U.S. Government Printing Office, 2000.

U.S. Senate, *Continuation of the Waco Investigation: Hearing Before the Subcommittee on Administrative Oversight and the Courts of the Committee on the Judiciary*. Washington, DC: U.S. Government Printing Office, 2001.

Index